Perpetual Search

Nkwazi Nkuzi Mhango

Langaa Research & Publishing CIG
Mankon, Bamenda

Publisher:
Langaa RPCIG
Langaa Research & Publishing Common Initiative Group
P.O. Box 902 Mankon
Bamenda
North West Region
Cameroon
Langaagrp@gmail.com
www.langaa-rpcig.net

Distributed in and outside N. America by African Books Collective
orders@africanbookscollective.com
www.africanbookscollective.com

ISBN-10: 9956-764-31-0

ISBN-13: 978-9956-764-31-0

Table of Contents

Acknowledgments

To my wife Nesaa and our children Nthethe (ka), Ndiza, Ng'ani, Nkuzi and Nkwazi Jr. Thanks so kindly; you have always been inspirational to me.

My friends, Professors Sean Byrne and Mnyaradzi Mawere, Sisters, Roselyne, Philo Ikonya; and Brother Salih Hassan Ibrahim, you, too, have shaped my way of doing things in various capacities and ways.

Thanks once again. Altona Library provided me bliss for meditating, researching and writing. Joanna Woods worked on the review expediently and professionally. This is my fourth poetry that Woods reviewed. I wholeheartedly thank her.

Introduction

Perpetual Search is a nerve-numbing piece of poetry that challenges all humans. The odes here want everybody to ask themselves who they think they are. So, too, it explores the human nature based on both sides of the coin of the exemplification of human comportment. It is the pursuit aimed at interrogating some human behaviours and practices that, are sometimes, taken for granted despite having indelible impacts on people's lives. Of all, it is about the quest for aptness, communitas, love, happiness, power, wealth, life without questioning how they are attained. The second sonnets chide those who portray themselves as leaders challenging them and the ruled to embark on a search for a better life for all by truly fighting corruption and searching for the *holier than thou*. Third limericks are about protecting mother earth seriously and practically. The last couplets take readers back to normal life that some–if not all–go through. It is about marital relationship not to mention the call on Illegal Immigrants, Song of Africa, Poetry as a Weapon and The Lost Hope.

Essentially, *Perpetual Research* is a philosophical quest that raises questions that seem to be simple but are in fact difficult. All of all, the book is built on the quest for human desire based on search for better life and perfection.

Perpetual Search

I call upon everybody everywhere
Everybody please come closer
I've something important to natter
So, everybody lend me you ear
I am coming with the quest for a search
It is from this milieu
That I want everybody to reach
So, too, I want to teach
Then I have to learn first

As blind and as fallible humans are
As smart we may think we are
Even if we are not
Are we really smart?
Aren't we mere mortals?
Yes, we are
If this we know
Then why are we playing *holier than thou*?
Aren't we on transit?
Do we know where we are heading?
Do we know what for us is waiting?
This being the truth
Why do we cling to things?
Are we going to go with such things?
Didn't we come nude?
Yes, we did
Aren't we wonders on earth?
Truly we are
Despite everything being clear
Humans will never admit that

We're always in a search

I always see people in a search
Yes, they are in a perpetual search
Indeed, the many are on the search
I can see everybody embarking on the search
Yes, I can see many people searching
They, indeed, are searching for many things
They are always searching for various things
Yes, different things
The search always dings
What a search without end!
When will it end?
Nobody can exactly tell

Life is about the search
Some people are searching for wealth
Even if it means robbing others
Even those who are rich still search
Have they ever been satisfied with their wealth?
Not on this material world
Where greed has become a creed

Some exploit the poor
Their lives are purely in glamour
Wealth has always been their clangour
They don't care
They are as greedy as a condor
They see and seek nothing but grandeur
This is the only thing in the valour
All people of every colour

Wealth has turned everybody into its prisoner

Life has many things to offer
Also there are many trends to follow
All depends on one's behaviour
Some steal from their countries' coffers
Others torment their families
All they want is wealth
Some forget even their health
Immense is the search for the wealth
What an unending search!

While some people are in chaos
As they run after wealth
Some are in search for peace
Yet, war becomes their means
Others use violence
They end up in chaos
The search becomes even messy
When others commit injustices
Some seek justice
Yet, they don't do justice
They seek just for themselves
Even by denying the same for others
You wonder; what type of justice this is
That never considers others
I cannot understand this justice
It acts selectively
Again, do they attain perpetual peace?

Some seek solace
Even if it means disturbing others
Some seek stability
Even if it means destabilising others
Others seek romance
Even if it means offending others
This is the search I see
That has always claims its victims

Some seek academic successes
Even if they know they are incompetent
They resort to cheating
I see the many showering themselves praises
As they move around with their fake titles
They aim at looking great
Even if they know they are minute
Their target is greatness
Even if it is fake prominence
They will still pursue it

Others seek harmony and comfort
Others venture into the spiritual world
While others still seek mundane feats
Some want everything fortified
Yet, they make others diffident
Sometimes, you don't get it
As to which is which in this search?
What a search!
The search without end

Humans invented weapons
All they seek is security

Nations amass dangerous weapons
Armies are always at alert
They are ready to fight
If you ask what they fight for
You don't get anything meaningful
For, they still suffer from insecurity
Isn't this insanity?

Some countries pay armies more money than doctors
If you ask what the duo does
You don't get any logic
Yet, this is how it is
Those whose role is to kill
Wonder; they are more taken care of
Than those whose role is to cure

Humans have invented all sorts of gadgets
Even those they don't need or want
Yet, they still spend billions of money
All they need is serenity
Have they ever attained it?
I bet
What they attained is nothing but want
Are they content?
I bet
They sadly are not

I saw people seeking beauty
They do it through ugly things

They do weird and crazy things
Some go through lots of pangs
When you ask the meaning of beauty

You end up getting many different things
Beauty keeps on eluding you all along
While it fascinates others
Some don't breastfeed their babies
All is done to keep the beauty
Isn't this injustice to babies?
Ironically, the world has consented to criminality
What beauty is this?
That comes by the way of injustices?

Beauty has deceived the many
I see women enlarging their extremities
Others increase their breasts
All they seek is beauty
They even don't fear cancers
They spend thousands carelessly

I have evidenced others destroying their colour
Whiteness has become another holy grail
All sorts of lighteners are applied
Those behind it want to look white
When you ask them about this self-discrimination
You will be told it is a fashion
A fashion!
Is it not an abomination?

Some are aware of their searches
Some know nothing about their searches

Yet, they all are equally in the search
The search for self-fulfilment
Is it fulfilment of self-belittlement?
Will there be any fulfilment in human life really?
I doubt
I am sorry about saying that
Again, that is that
Should I say as keen as we are?
Or as desperate as we are
This is why we're on a search

Let me concentrate on the search
We're searching for who we are
For, we know where we are
Yet, we know nothing about the future
We're searching above and beneath
Yes, we're always in a search
A search for hidden truth
Indeed, everybody would like to grasp this truth
However, the truth has never availed itself
We are still on a search

I've some issues with truth
Whenever anything is called truth
There have been many truths though
The truth is always convoluted
The truth is always idiosyncratic
Truth is always chaotic
It has caused many miseries

What is this truth?
I've always found though

Truth has many meanings
Every truth is truth
However, it can mean many things
Truth lacks truthfulness
It is always murky and illusory
What an allegory!

Your truth is not my truth
So, too my truth isn't your truth
Yet, between us, there is a truth
How do we gauge this truth?
While everybody has his or her truth
Whose truth should we hold?
And, whose truth should we discard?

When it comes to truth
Power is a determinant
Power defines truth
So, too, it fabricates truth
Governments claim they have the truths
Religions have always created their truths
The duo have always been in bed
Yet, they all call their fabricated truths truth
Whatever they say they call it truth
Even if it is a fabricated untruth
It will be called truth
Again, is this really the truth?
Is it the ultimate Truth?
Is it the one that we all search for?

Power may be knowledge
The truth of an educated person isn't the same

To that of an uneducated person
The truth of an informed person
Is always different to that of the uninformed one
The truth of the doyen
Is different from the truth of the greenhorn
Tycoon's lie may be regarded as a truth
Pauper's truth may be deemed untruth
This is the power of defining truth
Almost all things follow this trend
However deceptive it may seem like
It still has the logic to make

Government's truth is different from that of the citizens
While government uses propagandas
Citizens have no propaganda apparatuses
Instead, the citizens chomp government's propagandas
You'll see this in government's agendas
It decides for the people
And it goes on saying its decision if for the people
And by the people!
Of the people
And for the people
What people?
Those with power
Or those on whom power preys?
What a fable!
Which people?
Real people or imaginary people

One of the truths we all accept is death
Is there anybody who disputes death?

We're all waiting for death
whenever it arrives we'll track
I'm informed with our search
That we all love life
This is the truth
Maybe, life and death
Are the only truths
Despite loving life
Yet, some commit suicide
Is our love of life a truth?
Or it leaves us divided

We all love life
Even those who commit suicide
They do so for the afterlife
Whether it is real or not
The fact is
We all love life

Some commit suicide to *go* to the heaven
Some do so because of confusion
Others tell other to commit suicide
Yet, they are afraid of death!
Yes, they are cowered before death
The one they teach other not to fear

We'd like to know why we die
For, whenever someone dies we cry
Do we really need to cry?
Ironically, we don't question why we live
We don't quest why we were born
Is it our given right to live?
I doubt

It is a gift
If yes, from whom?
Please don't ask me

How many died in their early ages
Did they have this right to relish?
We consult the power that's most high
Everybody entrusts it with his or her life with love
We conventionally call this power God
Yet, we are still in search
Where is this God
The one that doesn't respond
Where is this God
That depends on the mortals

Some doubt about the presence of God
They'd like to see him or her
Yet, nobody has ever seen God
Never
Some say "if you see God you'll die?"
Others say they saw God
When you ask how they did
They end up saying different things
Moses is said to have *seen* God
Yet, he said he saw fire
Is God fire?
Jacob wrestled with God!
Whom he called nocturnal
Jacob defeated God
He forced him to bless him
What God was this?

That an Oldman Jacob beat?

Is this the God of injustices?
The one who offered Palestine's' land to others?

Why didn't this God see justice?
Is this the same God who spoke in Arabic?
Is this the God who blessed deserts?
As he cursed paradises available in Africa
What a god that happens to be referred as God!
The god of neo-religions
Everybody prays to him or her
Yet, nobody had her or him to hear
Search has been going on and on
Nobody can prove what he or she claims
Fable has always stood before, between or among us

I have never stopped wondering
How can God condone injustices?
How could God be blind of clear justice?
Is this real God?

I always defend the God of Ubuntu
The one who made all of us equals
This God has no infidels
Neither does this God has gentiles
Everybody is equal
This is God
The one and only God
Everybody needs to listen to

This is the God of forgiveness

The one who made Africans forgive their tormentors
It is only this God of justice
That taught Africans not to discriminate against others
It is this sole God with all qualities of purity and greatness
This is God of truthfulness

Others are but fake ones

I am going back to truth
Our truth is like sugar and bile
Think about it for a while
Some love sugar
Others love things that are bitter
Yet, they all seek satisfaction
Then, what is this satisfaction?

When I look at how people eat pepper
I just but wonder
What is it that is in pepper?
That makes some people love pepper

You can go as far as interrogating colours
What makes us choose some as we abhor others?
Which colours are truly good?
And which are truly debauched
Is something bad real *bad*?
Is something good really *good*?
What is bad for you may be good for me
And what is good for you may be bad for me

Some assign colours gendered roles
They say pink is for the girls

Where is the ink for girls?
To me, this is nothing but mere hyperboles
Some associate colours with sexuality
Others associate them with nativity
Others go further associating them with productivity

However everybody is entitled to making choices
Why should choose for others?
Who told them that boys can't wear pink?
Let's try to think
Do we need to be defined by the colours of our dresses?

Should we go for what shines in the light or what is hidden in
the dark?
Shining things may deceive more than hidden ones
Again, aren't we stuck in the dark?
Aren't we ignorant of the accuracy?

Everybody is truly in search
Yes, eternal search
We are equally in search
Searching for the truth

This search makes us equal
Nobody is smarter than another
Some deceive others
They pretend to know more
Once they go back to their sheaths
They face a stark reality for sure
Do they actually know what they claim?

You want to be cared for
Yet, you don't care about others
Life is about reciprocity
Failure to this is irresponsibility
Why don't you act first?
Instead of demanding first

Some want to be where they've never arrived
They want to be seen differently from what they actually are
They live in lies, pipedreams and falsehoods
They like to be great even if they're low-grade
One must be what he or she is
This is what enlightenment is all about

It is better to know where one's going
Than living wishing to be what you aren't
It is better to be simple
Then be upheld
Than self-aggrandisement
To end up in embarrassment

Some seek money to attain happiness
Can money fix broken hearts?
Can money heal inner wounds?
Is money all we need?
Animals are sometimes happy
Yet, they don't have any money
I once saw a monkey
She was playing with her baby
She, indeed, was happy
Yet, she didn't have money
So far, she didn't have any dynasty

Neither did she have a dray
Did she participate in the search?
I doubt
How'd she while she was satisfied?

Wealth has hijacked human search
Everyone wants to it to latch
Everybody would like it to clutch
Some sell drugs to get money
Others sell their bodies to get money
Others sell their countries
Yet, they die without happiness

Many suffer from their guilty
Others pretend they are innocent
In the backs of their minds and hearts
They weep and suppurate
Their activities affect the whole society
Yet, they have never gotten it
That money can never win them piety

Criminals are flocking the churches
You'll see them in the mosques
They serve two worlds
Will they run away from themselves?
Whom are they fooling besides themselves?
How many do you know?
Of course, so many

Thugs are in the search for money
They only depend on their felony
Once they get the same money

They still long for normalcy

Some countries sell weapons
Yet, they preach peace
If you ask them what this is
No answer will ever come forth
Shall there come any
Of course they will say
"No war no peace!"
Isn't this hypocrisy?

We are all searchers
We are all in doubts and fears
Don't we love life and fear death
Yet, we have some of us
Those are ready to die even for nonsense
Are such people smart or senseless?
Who is different from all of us?
Don't we hate each other for baloneys?

I can't help but wonder
Seeing people loving death
I thought they have no fear
Yet, one can aver
They don't fear death out of fear
Yes, they fear their master
Fear is fear
Whether you fear death or your master
Fear is fear

Fear is fear
He who fears death has fear

He who loves death, too, has fear
Yes, the fear of his manipulator
The fear of his derided master

Whatever we do is a search
Some search for love
Yet, they hate others
Others search for eternal life
While they know it is but a belief
Others search for wealth
Even if it means death
Yet, many forget happiness
By just ending up in a mess
Other end with a self-curse

Isn't a happy pauper better than a tycoon?
A health pauper is better than a sick queen
How many think this way?
How many avoid material sway?
A health dog is better than a sick master
They all need dear life
This is their search

Yes, we need life
Is life without a purpose meaningful?
Some complain a lot about life
Yet, they don't want to die
However, they die

We all need love
We need to be loved
We need to have everything we need

Yet, we end up losing everything we desired
Let me talk about love
What is this love?
Is love without foundation meaningful?
Why'd you want to be loved while you hate others?
Why'd you want to live longer while you kill others?
Why'd you become richer while you are mean?
Do you care about the poor?
Don't others rob the poor?
As those in power
Some came from poor families
Today they are moguls
Ask them how they made their wealth
They robbed the poor
Some are mere thugs
They kill and mug
Ironically, they want to be love
They want to live forever
How?

All this is a search
Everything we do is nothing but a search
We search differently
Some do so honestly
Others do so dubiously
They end up being duped
Others end up being disillusioned

We are all on a search
We search above and beneath
Never shall we stop this search
It is only when we breathe the last

The search will always be extant

You can't always be a winner
Otherwise you are a no-brainer
If you were a thinker
You'd accept becoming a loser
Sometimes, a winner is a loser
And a loser can become a winner
Losing isn't a misnomer
Victory is not a factor

Aren't we blind despite having eyes?
Aren't we deaf despite having ears?
We make many mistakes
Some are even timid
Yet, we don't comprehend
Why do we do what we do?
If you look at the mess
The whole world is now in
You'll understand what I mean
Look at violence
Consider sheer misunderstandings
Think about battles
Look at corruption
Look at bigotry
Look at selfishness
Aren't these signs of or blindness
Who do this?
Aren't they humans
Will they live forever?
Aren't they unaware?

They are
Again, what do they actually do?
Some repeat the same

Everybody wants to look good
Even if he or she looks bad
Many do bad things
Yet, they want to be deemed as good
Even those who do bad things
Do want good things
They want to be appreciated
They want to be respected
For what should they be appreciated?
For what should they be respected?
Aren't such people blind?
Aren't they confused?

Evil doers are blind
Most of them are fraidy-cats
Yet, they think they are astute
So as to be celebrated

Others want wealth
Despite not working hard
Others want peace
They do so through wars
Can violence beget peace?
What type of peace is this?
Haters want to be loved
Haters will always be haters
Never shall they become something else
Love so that you can be loved

If you hate you will be hated
This is the canon rule

Look at preachers
They urge us to love poverty
They make heaven ridiculous
For, they make it look synonymous with poverty
Sometimes, I don't get it
For, they preach poverty
However, they are themselves opulent
They get the money from poor believers
Are such bilkers different from robbers?
They con poor believers
Who don't ask why preachers are rich
Ironically, they say the heaven is for the poor
Don't we see this denial?
Isn't this a double standard?
Who takes on them?

Jesus was a pauper
I know this for sure
Wasn't he next to a beggar?
Where did he get the coin to pay tax?
Didn't he pay Caesar?
Do you think it was a hoax?
Didn't he get the money from the fish's gut?
The disciples had a fish to coax
Now, we need to ask
Why are preachers tycoons?

I know many preach Jesus' gospel
They claim they are Jesus' disciples

Jesus was homeless
Why do they live in mansions?
Do they preach the words of Jesus?
Or just preach their greed and lusts

Sinners want to be regarded as angels
Where will we put the archangels?
Thieves don't want to be robbed
Yet, they rob others
Aren't they sightless?
He who robs others
He'll be robbed
It is the matter of time
He gets what he deserves
This is the search

How many killers do you know?
Where are they
How many did they kill before being killed?
How many did they hang before being hanged?
Live by sword die by sword
This is the result of the search

How many innocent people are rotting in jail?
Aren't the criminals free?
Where is justice?
Where is fairness?
Indeed, it is a search
The search for everything

Sometimes, the search turns murky

Everything becomes gloomy
Sinners judge the innocent
Thieves are entrusted the bank
The frail are given power
We see them in power
They deem themselves powerful
You don't get it
It is an upside-down thing
It is always confusing
Yet, it is a search

Fire can boil water and dry it
Doesn't water douse fire?
Which is which here?
Wisdom is always like that
It can be used both ways
When it used rightly
It is called wisdom
When it is used wrongly
It is called folly

How do you go to heaven by denying others the same?
How do you realise such a dream by blocking others?
We'd all like to go the heaven
How'd you go to heaven?
While you live like a heathen

This, indeed, is a search
Everybody needs to search
Especially in our hearts
The hearts of hearts

Do I deserve what I want?
Why should I get all that?
While what I do is different?
Let us do others justice
Before wanting justice from ourselves

Let's keep on the search
It's something for us to teach
Essentially, we're own classes
We thus, must look at ourselves
We've all lessons within ourselves

Indeed, human life is about a search
It has a very good hunch
It entirely depends on one's approach
There are those who want happiness
By denying others the same happiness
Others use their powers as a weapon
Others use their money as a bludgeon
Such people need to keep on the search
To know what they are required of

The quest for happiness is huge
It's always been a struggle
For some it is but a kerfuffle
For others it is a gamble
Some kill in order to be happy
Some do sad things in order to happy
Yet, you ask yourself
Many things baffle
What is happiness?

Some drink liquor to be happy
Others smoke marijuana to be happy
Yet, they end up being unhappy
What a fable!
They become flummoxed
For, they don't get what they need
Everything becomes convoluted

Some exploit others to achieve happiness
They careless about others' happiness
Others control others to achieve peace
They detain others to achieve freedom
Their freedom is a doom for others
You can see this in patriarchy setting
Aren't female suffering?

A man wants a pious wife
Yet, he elopes with other ladies
Even the one with many wives
He wants them to be pious
While he is impious

A wife loves her relatives
Then he hates her husband's relatives
Can such folly work really?

Look at heartless and deplorable honour killings
Aren't females in some communities suffering?
Their deaths are the happiness of the killers
Where is females' honour?
Aren't they owned and exploited
Aren't they objectified?

Ironically, some say they do that for God!
Is it for God or for dogs?
Even dogs don't kill each other
Just to honour each other

Along happiness is perfection
Many aspire for perfection
Everybody would like to be seen as perfect
Yet, for the matter of fact
Nobody is perfect
And nobody will ever be perfect

Some kill and torture others
Yet, they end up in a quagmire
Many don't even worry
They want to get what they aspire
They don't even bother
To think about others
Theirs is important
Others' don't matter

As selfish as such creatures are
They think they deserve justice
They think they deserve love
How when they don't care about others?
How if they don't look beyond their noses?

Some seek beauty
Many chemicals are bought
Mirrors take a centre stage
Yet, all is but a mirage
Fake beauty is no beauty

Why can't they accept who organically they're?

Some seek to define beauty
Leading in this is the West
All want to look smart
The beauty will always be in the hunt
They end up with burns and welts
Yet, they don't stop this self-inflicted calamity

You'll see them with burnt faces
Nevertheless, others don't want to learn
They just repeat the same fallacy
As if they have no eyes

Pride is another thing that many seek
Wealth and education take a lead
We have never stopped the search
Yet, it has never been in our reach

Some seek to be strong
Either peacefully or by a violence
Again, all along
Everybody has feebleness
The stronger are weak
And the weak may become stronger

I see some talking about justice
Yet, to others, they do injustices
Others talk about humanity
While theirs is inhumanity
Such people need to embark on search
Life is about search

Some are educated
Nonetheless, they act as illiterates
Others are gifted
Nevertheless, they abuse their talents
We are all on a search
There is somewhere we want to reach
There is a lesson to learn
There is an experience to gain

Some are very energetic
Yet, they have no anger
Others are choleric
Theirs is full anger

Imagine if the bull would be easily provoked
Or if Chihuahua had such power
We need to research whodunits
In order to avoid myths

Can the mountain wish it were a valley
Or the valley wish it were a mountain
They all have a host of tribulations
The mountains suffer from the Sun
The valleys suffer from the rain

The mountain is always barren
The valley is always fertile
Yet, they both depend on each other
They perfect each other
None can live without another
None is better than another

Buffalo, elephants and wildebeest eat grasses
Don't grasses feed on them?
Ask them
Where do their carcasses go?
If they are not eaten by hyenas and lions
They end up rotting to become manure for grasses

Crocodiles and monitors lay eggs
Eagles, too, lay eggs
Yet, they eat others' eggs
Not knowing theirs will also be eaten
Doesn't monitor steal crocodile's eggs?
Isn't there any wisdom in this?

Birds have no houses
They live in cages
Others build nests
They might have more happiness
Than those who live in castles
There are those who are gifted
They have money yet unused
To the contrary, others have children
However, they've no money to feed them

The search has always gone on
Nobody knows its culmination
We seek various things
By doing various things

Some things searched for are nonsensical
Other things we aspire are illogical

However, all have a rationale
Why victimising others
For the quest of your pipedreams

Victimisation among us has been going on
Though, it has never brought any solution
We're always repeating the same mistakes
Everything is at stake

Despite committing all atrocities
The society still agonises
Why can't we search for change?
Instead of maintain carnage

For search of peace others go to war
Can war bring peace really?
If it can it is but a half-full jar
The end product of war is butchery

Some feel happy when they see blood
They kill others like animals
They are always proud
That they have won battles!

Human life is sickening
It is always confusing
However, sometimes, it can be rewarding
We still have a long way to go
To get out of our manmade no-go
Everybody needs mettle
To get out of one's ego

Our ego is one of the factors
That let some of us become monsters
Egotism is a great sinister
Many look at themselves
While they ignore others
If you don't care about others
Don't expect them to care about you

Our search has two protagonists
They encounter each other in many aspects
There are winners who are males
There are losers who are females
However, this is based on gender rationales

Some seek dominance as means of happiness
Others seek subservience as means of bliss
Such are ready to be used by others
They allow themselves to be tools for others
Humiliating as it is
They still see it differently
They allow themselves to become hopeless
Like sheep, they don't query
Like dogs, they don't rebel
Winners enjoy their domination
While losers suffer under subordination

Again, we need to ask
What is this life that puts us at risk?
We need to answer this question
Maybe, we'll get a solution
Whatever answer we'll get

Maybe, will expand our vision

Despite living on terrains
Humans have never been satisfied
They look upon the heavens
So as to communicate with God
Have they ever found God!
God knows

Bob Marley put it well
He made a good query
"Many people like to go to the heaven,
Yet, they are not ready to die"

Everybody wants to enter the paradise
For many it is by wishes not performances
They know what they do are mere lies
Yet, they call it high!

Knowing their blatant blindness
God has maintained silence
God left everything to them
In the end, it has become mayhem

We create myths
We turn them into realities
We embark on faiths
Now, they've become calamities

We're always on a search
Searching for answers
Many laws we make and break

Yet, we get no answers

We've invented many gadgets
All are aimed at happiness
Yet, we're still hijacked
In our messes we are trapped

We invented all sorts of weapons
To beef up our security
Yet, many die of the same weapons
You wonder
What type of security is this?

We invented all sorts of medicines
To fight and curb diseases
Yet, we still have them to abuse
Looking at this
I end up baffled!

Many seek solace
As they aspire for peace
Some are tired of peace
They envisage violence

We search for equality
Yet, others claim superiority
They want to be above all
Without knowing this is foul

We pretend to love creation
Yet, we embark on obsession
Xenophobia

Gynophobia
Islamophobia
Blackophobia
Transphobia
Afrophobia
West-phobia
Europhobia
Egoism
Sexism
Racism
Misogyny
Phobia, phobia, phobia

Life has panoply of intricacies
Everything good is in deficiency
While everything bad is in abundance
Interestingly, we call this normalcy!

We dictate everything
However, we are dictated
Those you think are above everything
Sometimes, they ironically are subjugated
Some present themselves as masters
In actuality, they have hidden masters
Go ask your leaders
If they beg
They must have masters
What have you found?

Do kings rule over their wives?
Do queens lord it over their spouses
They are above the dominion

Yet, they are under someone's inspiration
Kings' wives tell them what to do
They comply like dogs
Who is the ruler here?
Between the king and the queen

When the baby is born,
It starts its search
It keeps its eyes open
To grasp what comes out of the search
It grows to a mature person
Then, it assumes its responsibilities

The quest still doubles
The baby finds that there is no station
If anything, it is only troubles
The creature starts the struggles

A tycoon wants to live forever
So too, does the pauper
They, yet, all surely die
They'll never stop making a sigh

Some decide not to eat meat
They think it is cruelty to animals
Yet, they eat plants
Isn't that cruelty to plants?

Some drink no liquor
Yet, they abuse other things
What they need is a stupor
They do all kinds of things

All aiming at being happy

Humans are complicated indeed
You can see this in their choices
Nobody will ever be satisfied
Sometimes, life becomes chaos
However, we like differences
Occasionally, they ruin us
People differ and hate others
Why can't we come together?
Why can't we negotiate the differences?
Let's mitigate our dissimilarities
Let's accept our weaknesses

However, humans are subject to change
Change is always for whoever wants to change
We can change the way we do things
We can change the way we perceive things
What is needed is true change

Doing the same with the same unfavourable results is not
change
Change must be aspired for the improvement of one's life
and others'
Nobody can escape interdependence and interconnectedness
We are all connected; and we're always embarking on change
Facing and taking on change can be in itself change

Change is always around
Though time doesn't wait for us
So, it is always upon us and only us
To search for this wad

Life is about; and revolves around search
Yes, we search for different and many things
Somethings are on our reach
While others are completely out of our reach
Again, we will never stop the search
Yes, living is about the search

Of all things we search for
Number one is our thirst
Can we satisfy it?
How do we coexist with it?
Should we accept to be taken by our desires?
Or, should we arrest our desires

Billionaires still search for more money
Paupers hope one day they'll get money
What a torturous journey!
Is the money the end of all?
Is it an end in all?
Or the end in itself
Or just the beginning of all

Sometimes, we live as if we'll never die
Yet, we consequently die
From time to time, it is good to live like that
Especially, when we harvest
For, we produce many products
Although, we leave them abaft

When it comes to being good
We better live like birds on trees

For, we have nothing good
That we can take to our graves

It is only our good deeds
But not material things
Let's balance our search
We can somewhere reach

Life has tricked us
Though we think we enjoy it
Hasn't it enslaved us?
If not,
Why do we run after it?

We talk of joy
We talk of success
Is there any joy
Wherein others are amiss
Joy is societal
But not individual

Our lives are like a rainbow
Nobody will ever tame it
Try to chase the rainbow
You will never catch it

Again, when the rainbow is gone
We realise in an admiration
It was but a delusion
It has no face or dimension

I'd like to pose a question

Have you ever asked this question?
What's the purpose of your lifespan?
If at all you live in rejection
How did you manage to live that longer?
Is it within your power?
Do you know what is behind it?
You may boast of your wealth
But you cannot boast about your lifespan
People are able to make money
But they cannot elongate their ages
They can build castles
But they cannot decide how long
They will live in these castles?

I understand some people build castles
They do it as if they'll live in them forever
Despite seeing others as they suffer
Even by living in hovels
Do they get any lesson?

They say their performances aren't our business
We're winners
They're losers
Everybody minds her or his business
We end up in crimes

Thieves see theft as a form of justice
And indeed, for them it is justice
Yet, for others it is injustice
Simply because they're missing out of the deal
This is especially in politics
Robbing others for others is but peace

Rejecting it is violence
You'll be told you're disturbing peace
Especially when you refuse
You don't allow others to rob in peace
Yes, their peace is your violence
Maybe, your peace, too, is their violence
When you refute their joysticks
They will pour vitriols
Disorderly conduct they will call

Again, when you consider how they pursuit power
Yes, political power
They become humbler
They plead and court
Once they get the power
They change and become the masters-cum-monsters
The ones you used to rub shoulders with
End up becoming unreachable and *holier than thou*

Everything is forgotten
Once elections are done
Your friendships abruptly come to a sudden end
The search then has to begin
You wonder why
Why being maltreated this way
Why being avoided
This is politics anyway

In the search for power
A hyena becomes a dove
You'll evidence hyenas and monitors as they cower
They'll pretentiously show love

Once they get the dear power
Police replace love
Requests become commands
Orders become laws
Put it this way
Go back to heydays
When a couple get married
They expect to fly high
Expectations are always tall
Once they start life after
Things start to change
Whatever that they envisaged
Start to become fifty-fifty
Some even regret
Other decide to stay put
Always life is like that
Nobody can predict it

While some regret their decisions
Others are craving to be married
While other are exiting marriage
Million are entering the institutions
Life, indeed, is like a mirage
Nobody knows it well

Some of those in marriage are struggling
While other are cherishing
Again, is marriage such a bad or good thing?
All depends on your analysis
To some, marriage is a paradise
To others, the same is an abyss
Again, everything is still a search

Some pray vigorously to have children
Others were tortured by their own children
Indeed, life is a search
It is a search full of headache
Despite its hitch
Nobody abandons the search

Some say they believe in God
They add that they depend on God's protection
Yet, they carry weapons!
Who is their protector between their God and their weapons?
Isn't this fallacy and confusion?

Some preach giving
Yet, they practice receiving
Whom are they deceiving?
Aren't they included in this deception?
Isn't what they're doing dupery based on exploitation?
How many of this type have you ever heard and seen
Many, many more everywhere

They exploit others out of their misdeeds
Don't we have the same needs?
You blatantly ignore my needs
Yet, you want me to meet your deeds
What fallacy!
The hypocrites preach wine and drink water

Does it need a tutor to appreciate my needs?
You better consider your deeds
Instead of acting like birds

Birds reap where they didn't sow
What do birds sow?
After attacking the farm
At least, birds leave manure abaft
What do preachers leave abaft?
After swindling the sinners?

A thief is a thief even if he or she steals by consent
It becomes even worse when the victims are ignorant
How many do you see in our streets?
Those enslaving and exploiting the indigents
Many, of course
Are such sinners the people of God?
Which God is this?
Whom conmen and women can tease
Don't they play God?

Why inculcating fear in others to get your cash
Why dupe others to get your wealth
Is there anybody who'll die with cash?
Once you are dead, you just become but trash
How many know this reality?

I know you need money
Yes, everybody needs money
Every bee loves honey
Yet, it doesn't deny other bees
The same right of enjoying honey

I am talking to people of power
Yes, those whose power is others' disaster
They lie that they believe in God

While wealth is their only God
Weren't you told of the rich man?
The heaven is not for rich men or women
The heaven is not for gluttons
The heaven is for pious ones
The heaven is for the poor!

How do you pray for someone while you need to be prayed for?
Prayers are for the dead for they lost their power
Prayers are for justice but not for dupery
How many do understand this this way?
Aren't swindlers dead morally?
Do they have the power to pray for anybody?

Wisdom is the venue of a few
But greed is the sanctuary for many
I am talking to you
You who has misled the many
Remember, there is a day
What will you say?
When your acts are put on the fair

You want to be heard
Even if you are not understood
Are you ready to listen?
Publicity makes a person proud
Yet, it becomes his cascade
We hear a lot of propagandas
Again, those behind them come to an end
This surely is the trend
Nobody will stand the test of time

You're dirty you want me to be clean
Clean your mess the teach me
Many are committing every sin
Yet, they want others to be holy
Can it work this way really?
It doesn't cross my brain
If it does, it is but a white tall tale
"Do as I Say" is a big white lie
It should not be done by humans
We all have eyes and brains
Why then dupe each other?
We need "Do as I do" but not "as I Say"

A good general is the one who leads the war
A coward is the one who declares war
While he stays at home
To be the witness while others face misfortunes
A brave man must be in the front
The enemies to confront
Staying back is an affront
It should not be done by humans

I love the hornets
Heroic as they always are
They're always at the forefront
They fight every war
Whether they lose or win
It has never been their concern

Aren't these tiny creatures wiser than many humans?
Yes, they're wise than kings and queens

Those who declare whatever wars
Yet, they cowardly remain in their towers

I love mother birds
They don't eat before their chicks
They first feed the chicks
Even if it takes them many loads
They'll honestly deliver the foods

Human leaders are totally different
Most of them eat first
They careless about the majority
For them, justice is for them to eat first!

How many do you know?
I know you know
They're many more everywhere
The righteous ones are nowhere
Jesus died a poor man
Even when he needed a coin
He had to catch a fish
He wasn't a tycoon
If it was worth he'd have been
When I see those who preach his doctrine
I just but grin
Do they believe in his canon?
If they don't why then
If anybody believes in him then
Many serving in his place would not have been

Whom are they cheating?
Isn't this self-cheating

Isn't this a sin?
Let's however move on
I hope point's been taken
Wow!
Let's keep on searching
The search for unearthing villains

Jesus came for sinners
Above all, he came for sufferers
His were orphans, widows and losers
Rainmakers and tycoons weren't his
Biblical Zacchaeus is a living instance

If you ask those false prophets
Who are they for apart from their pockets?
Aren't they the prophets of pockets?
Aren't they money changers of today?
Aren't many churches dens
Where thieves congregate
To make a killing

It makes me feel sick
I hate face masks
When I see gimmicks
Seeing muggers employing tricks
To rob innocent folks
Please talk the talk
Then walk the walk

Many castigate immorality
Isn't swindling people immorality
When it comes to prosperity

I saw many immoralities
People quote all editions of Bibles
They choose what is good for their duplicity
When it comes to the nitty-gritties
My foot!
It is all but deceit
Pay no hoot
It is all dupery

The *words* of God are on the market
All sorts of conmen are vending the gospel
They are making wealth out of poor people
They are making million fraudulently
They perform fake marvels
Are still there any miracles today?
Some even consult oracles
Poor people are openly pickpocketed
Governments pretend not to comprehend
They pretend to know nothing
Aren't they the same gang?
Aren't the thieves in the den?
Didn't Jesus Warn?
While politicians rob public coffers
Religious conmen rob paupers
They all play the same game
The difference is in their names

They forget that Jesus didn't write any Bible
They don't want to tell who wrote the bible
Congregations are not taught to question the bible
Do they know who wrote the bible?
So, too, Jesus didn't vend the ministry

Aren't our money makers vending the Bible?
Some tamper with the Quran

Did prophet Mohamad write the Quran?
Wasn't it written after his death?
Who questions the rationale of being written thereafter?
Some misconstrue it
They abuse his noble religion
They preach violence
Why can't they put sense?
Islam is peace!

If you want to live peacefully
Denounce violence
Preach justice and peace
Do you want security?
Stay away from wealth
Especially the one that's filth
You won't need any sentinel
You won't erect any tall wall
Poverty will secure you
Nobody will bother with you
Did Jesus have guards?
What for if he was pauper?

If you want to live piously
Stay away from violence
Keep off from zealotry
Preach love and peace
Just like the prophets did
Just like the Son of Man did

How many are ready to live like this
How many are ready to live like Jesus
I will tell you this
If we're to make people declare allegiance
You'd really wonder
Many of those preaching Jesus' gospel
Would miss out of this exercise

Jesus knew everything
Didn't he tell his people?
Many will come in sheep's clothing
And they will misled the many
Hyenas will be called lambs
They will devour many lambs
Is it hard to know hyenas in sheep's clothing
Believe ye me I tell you
Many won't only mislead you
Essentially they'll vend you
Do you remember Judas Iscariot?
How many Judas Iscariots do you dine with?
Haven't you given them the mettle?

Please embark on a search
Explore all I have said
Never stop the search
Expand it far to reach
You'll learn a host of things
That you used to take for granted

My search now rests here
This doesn't mean it is the end

I hope you have something to add
Please think and ponder
I am sure many you will benefit

All those you used to take for granted
Have lessons for you to learn

A Trailblazer

Let me talk about politics
Yes, politics
However tricky politics is
It is in the center stage of our lives
Let me extend my search
Yes, let me on politics latch
I am on the search
Search for healthy politics

I address the *third world's* sufferers
They are searching for trailblazers
After being pissed off with evil rulers
I am one of these
Yes, this is my case
It is your case
Indeed, it is our case

We need faithful leaders
The ones that can deliver us
The ones that look like us
Those who understand us
Yes, these are the ones
They are the ones that we need
The ones that we must find
The ones we can trust

This task is not easy
For, good leaders are scarce
They are like a need in the haystack
Many are quacks

Seeking to vend their folks
They are but foxes
Yes, pure wolves
You can see them everywhere
They are not easy to trace
We need honest leaders
Yes, we are searching for leaders
We are tired of rulers

We've been grappling with swindlers
Those who ruin our coffers
Most of them are suited beggars
They are as reprehensible as scars
They have never felt guilty of being beggars
Whatever they get from begging
Most of it is stashed offshore
Our national debts always soar
The same *bêtes noirs* don't bother
At home they keep on stealing
They invite their consigliore
To join the table in merrymaking
While our people are suffering
They care about nothing
Theirs has always been partying
Our flesh they are eating
Our blood their drinking
Our toils they are gulping
It is time to embark on search
The search for leaders

This being the conundrum
I can see pandemonium

The search is our addendum
Therefore the search goes on
We will always keep on
To make sure we find the solution

We need competent leaders
Visionary and clean leaders
These are the individuals we want
The ones that we can trust
The ones free of rust
This search if for leaders
Those that must replace the rulers
We need the viziers
We are tired of liars
We are tired of betrayers
We are tired of self-seekers
Yes, this search is for leaders

We're searching for leaders
Yes, we're looking for deliverers
After becoming tired of rulers
We are tires of swindlers
Tired of self-seekers
Political quacks
Yet, corrupt sharks
The sharks in power

Lost as we are
Betrayed as we are
We, indeed, need leaders
We long for true leaders
Capable and honest leaders

We are tired of hyenas
We deserve to have leaders
The ones that we will hear
We are tired of fibbers
We are tired of pretenders
We need the leaders
The ones with burning desires
To fix our structures
Those who don't abuse our powers
The ones who don't poop in our offices

We need visionary leaders
The servants of the peoples
The ones and only ones
The ones who will understand us
The ones who will carry on with our search
The search for our deliverance
We need better life

We don't need shepherds
Most of them eat their herds
Since they brought their creeds
Many have suffered ever since
We don't need birdies
Those who ruin farmsteads
We don't want birds
Those who rest on trees
Once stone lands
They took to their heels

We need clean and honest leaders
The ones who will partake of our quest

With whom we will share our troubles
We are in the search for our fulfilment
The search for our development
Yes, the search for our liberty

We don't want pretenders
Cons that feed us with mere lies
Like mosquitos they suck our blood
Like knives they severe our bond
To purgatory they have us bound
Like frogs in the pond
They sing our beauty
Behind the curtain, they have us vended

We need liberators
The ones that can propel us to the future
We're sick and tired of conjecturers
We are tired of *man eaters*
We are tired of tricksters
We are fed up with self-seekers
We need leaders
The ones that understand our mission
The ones that will keep the search on
These are the ones we want and seek

We need hard workers
We are tired of lazy beggars
We need go-getters
But not blood suckers
We need trailblazers
Those who will see the future
Hard workers who'll tell us to work harder

We need visionaries not goons
We have had many buffoons
Time to divorce them is now
Let us embark on the search
The search for our betterment

We need leaders who respect themselves
The ones to pin hope on
We don't need the ones who feed as with lampoons
We abhor goons
Those who want silencing us
We fear those who treat us like baboons
Those who hide in cocoons
The cocoons of tribalism
Cocoons of cronyism
Cocoons of nepotism
Cocoons of regionalism
The cocoons of nihilism
Never will we make do with them

I call upon you men or women of the people
I am looking for humble people
People with a strong mettle

To whom pomp's never been their symbol
Those who always keep a low profile
Simplicity must be their style
They must prove they're reliable
I am talking to the presidents
Yes, the prime ministers
Come join in the search
Our perpetual search

Honourable Presidents
This eulogy-cum-admonishment is yours
Yes, I mean it to be totally yours
It aims at giving you some advices
It gives you some inputs
Please take my nuggets
At this time you are on helms
I know it truly overwhelms
I think you need our nuggets
So that you can govern us as we want
This is our perpetual search

Make our search yours
Work for us
Listen to us
Never take a ride of us
Neither should you ignore us
Please don't vend us
Or think about fooling us
Stand and stick with us
So that we can save our peoples

This tome is yours
Take and read is yours
Own it is yours
Yes, yours to work on
So that the nations can move on
Africa needs to move on

Take it from the doyen
Yes, I'm the one among many

The one offering his contribution
The contribution to all nations
Yes, it is a great contribution
Take it is a premonition
I talk of the nations of Africa

Take this tome as an appeal
Yes, an appeal to you all
Read it whenever you feel to
Keep it if you want to
I'm sure it has some nuggets
That can help us in our assignments
Of which one is a search
The search for leadership

Take it is a *magnum opus*
Yes, it is its sacred onus
It tasks all of us
Especially the victims
Let us stand magnanimously
To chart our own way

The tome has crucial nuggets
Take it as an impetus
Use it; you won't regret
Keep on the search
This is what I want to teach

Leaders are anointed ones
Yes, they are the ones
Thus, they should be the anointed ones
Instead of being the annoying ones
Leaders must stand firmly; and bring expected changes
They must deliver their countries from the cascades
Leaders must save countries from the abysses
They must have all needed answers
This is the essence of their power
They must arrest and address all damages
All anomalies that dog their constituencies

We are always in struggle
Yes, especially when we face such a debacle
The world has become but a bubble
For those who have never enjoyed free will

As human we are eventful
Sometimes, other things are in the horizon
Our plates are so full
Importantly, everything needs to be done
After everything done
People expect their leaders to deliver
Leaders who do not deliver
Are as barren as a rock
Once leaders fail to deliver
They cease to be leaders
One thing for them to do
Just honourably relinquish power
Let others take over
So that they can deliver

Real leaders don't cling to power
Once their constitutional terms are over
They willingly hand over the power
For, they know this for sure
Power is for the people
They heed the people
And above all
They trust the people
They respect their constitutions

We recently witnessed madness
Some rulers tampered with their structures
Constitutions were abused
Promised were not honoured
Such self-seekers must be boycotted
Power is for the peoples
Power is not for mongrels

True leaders listen to their people
They don't superimpose their egos
They follow people's ethos
True leaders are not winos
They always are servants
They fear being seen as bosses
They never lord it over their subjects
They know power is a trust
They treat is modestly
True leaders suffer from no rust
The rust of prosperity
The rust of enormity
They understand the search

Their search is about justice
Their deeds are for peace
True leaders don't employ violence
They do not labour under secrecy
They respect their constitutions
They honour their vows
They are not double-faced
True leaders don't need sycophants
They don't need abettors

Let me talk to Mr. or Mrs. President
Take this for a fact
Don't think people don't know you
Whenever they hugely trust you
Never let them down

Everybody watches you
All eyes are on you
They want you to deliver them
This is what you promised them
The time you courted them
You just looked like them
Will you remain the same?

You assured them you are reliable
This is what you told voters
Everything was sparkly
Voters subscribed to this openly
Again, all this remains relevant
When you respect your oath

Now you are at the helm
Are you going to maintain the same acme?
Are you going someone else to become
Please keep your promises
The ones you made in the campaigns

You said you're a hard worker
So, too, you are a thinker
Prove this merit
If you worked hard to acquire it
People want to see your ability
They want prosperity
Everybody wants that
Yes, this is what people want
A true leader must do just that

Coming to power is euphoria
It is wonderful aura
When your name was pronounced
Everybody vivaciously hailed
Euphoria can be myopia
It lives temporarily
What is needed is practicability
What is needed is dependability

Election process must be competitive
Everybody had an initiative
Everybody wants to carry the day
In the end, one carries the day
Again, many end up being carried away
Away to the horizon

You hear them as they complain
Whoever that comes to the office
Must go down to business
Let's deliver the mass

Honourable anointed one
All eyes are on you
Now the burden is on you
Don't become a burden
We have seen so many
They came to power sparking
Soon, they became but loads
The faith people had in them
Slowly, escaped them
Once voters have faith in you
You must make sure you
Show leadership
This tells the people
That you are the one
The one that will deliver everyone
The one that will lead people
Yes, you must lead the people
Lead them to the future

Never invoke blarney
When people ask for honey
Never treat 'em like a donkey
Which the master rides freely
Without any reciprocity

Elections burn a lot of dirty money

Voters wonder where some got the money
They see them buying votes like crazy
When they ask why
What were they buying with their money?
Yes, most of the money used is dirty
Much is gotten illicitly
I've no doubt about this reality
Criminals squander their money
They want to buy their way
Yes, way to authority

Even those whose policies are openly phoney
They do bank on their money
Good leaders bank on humility
The best are always above all with vivacity
They maintain their integrity
Yes, they keep their humility
Power doesn't climb into their heads
This is what our search is all about

A leader is an educator
Please never abandon this factor
A true leader must learn and teach
Again, he doesn't know everything
Yes, a leader is always a teacher
He or she must accept to be a learner
A leader must have what it takes
He or she must avoid becoming a ruler
People vote for leaders
As they abhor the rulers

A leader must be a disciplinarian

Must have the chutzpah to take actions
This is more important than thralldoms
Democracy and justice
Always define true leadership
A true leader is like a chip
That runs the system
When it comes to do justice
A true leader never looks into the eyes of simians
Those who corruptly want to create a mess
A leader takes the on mercilessly
Even if they are her or his relations

Leading is always a noble call
Surely, it is the noblest of all
Ruling is always artificial
Many rulers commit wrongs
Leaders do correct the wrongs
A true leader knows many wrongs
That sent her or his country under
A leader makes everything clear
To take a failed country back to its glory

I tell leaders of dependent economies
Please cure your economies
Use creativity and good alchemies
To revamp the economies
Apply impartiality
Invoke accountability
Embark on pellucidity
Revamp the economy
Use conviviality
Kicks start agronomy

Seek technology
Embark on taxonomy

For those endowed with resources
Put mechanisms in place
Make sure you enter good deals
Avoid all underhand dealings

Overhaul your systems
In order to discover the problems
Africa needs working systems
The systems that work for all

Our systems are corruptly jammed
They serve just a few
Those who are heinously connected
Many live in an economic curfew
As they grapple with poverty
Only a few frauds
Are swimming in prosperity
This anomaly can't go on

True leaders must bring solutions
True leaders know what brought Africa down
Surely, they know; it is nothing but corruption
They take corruption mercilessly head on
By all means and vigorously they fight corruption
They make sure the nations are free from exploitation
For, corruption has sank Africa
We need to search for the solutions
This is our search
A perpetual search

We all know what happened to our education
We still use colonial edification
We must embark on the decolonisation
We need some sort of invention
Let us claim back our education
That was slew many years ago
True leaders must revamp our education
They must resuscitate our institutions
They know who felled our education
So, too, they know how it was ruined
They need to work on strategies
To see to it we overhaul everything

Poor leadership has ruined us
We've become nations of thieves
Those who steal from themselves
Crooks think about deals
They have divorced ideas
All which used be ideal
Have been sent to hell
Nobody is thinking about the future
We can't go on with this conjecture
Somebody has to reign in
This is the leader

No country can develop without education
Yes, we need an educated nation
It is not just the matter of education
We need quality education
In order to compete in this century
We need well educated citizenry

Rejuvenate the culture of reading
Yes, now our people hate reading
Books are treated like garbage
While other baloneys are venerated
I see many drinking cages everywhere
This way we're going nowhere

Teachers need to be remunerated
All essentials must be provided
Students must be motivated
We must reward their effort
Nothing can purge this out
It is only through fighting graft

Instead of heavily investing in schools
Most of our people are investing in hotels
Others invest in brothels
This way we can't compete with others
We send our people abroad
Because our schools are not good
We need to revive the spirit of education
Yes, Africa as a nation
This must be our obligation

Promote creativity
Based on productivity
Punish mediocrity
Don't reward loyalty
Do everything with sincerity
I'm sure we'll gain velocity
Everybody must fulfil his responsibility

This is when we can expect prosperity

Many countries went to the dogs
Yes, we behave like cyborgs
When we see such a forgery
We need true leaders to take on this chicanery
Aren't our bigwigs are involved in forgery?
It indeed makes me feel sorry
When we're compared to dogs

Go to many African parliaments
Are they pregnant with doctors?
Professors
Go-getters
Again, when you look at their achievements
You see nothing but resentments

Sometimes, it makes sense
Surely, it causes annoyance
Again, seeing ministers who are forgers
And still they remain ministers
Such ministers should be fired
Thereafter, they'd be charged
This will send a signal
To all types of criminals

I know there are a couple of doubters
They see politicians as schemers
True leaders must see it coming
Instead of scheming or complaining
True leaders must see nothing wrong
Instead, they must deliver

Our search tells me one thing
We need to keep the embers burning
People need to keep countries going
This is what people are hoping
Leaders must give them hope
Leaders must have people to prop

Leaders are officially been appointed
Yes, they are always anointed
Our votes create our leaders
In return, we hope to get good services
We're tired of lip services
Elections bring euphoria
For the most hope is always higher
So, too, expectations are indeed high
Africa is searching for a select few
Who will propel it to the future?

A leader must build bridges
He or she puts heads together
For the building of the nation
Looking at the mess we are now in
It must attract real leaders' attention
As the moment sets in
We hope our leaders would employ their experience
Such leaders need to have resilience
To take on all menaces people face

While other created networks for power
True leader display real power
They provide leadership

They steer the ship

Leaders must be cautious
They don't invest in ceremony
Every leader must be to serve the country
Yes, such take must benefit the country
Leader leads from the front seat
A leader doesn't lead from abaft

A true leader forms a good team
That must comprise of people with decorum
A leader must overhaul the whole system
He or she brings a lost glamour
I can hear people's clamour
I can hear their clangour
Yes my dear leader,
"Take on the current rotten system
Yes, the one that's brought us to the doom"
When people still have faith in you
Please never let them down

To any true leader,
The challenges are many
Look at the economy
It is sick and shabby
It needs someone to revamp it
Seriously fight graft
Everything will be spiffy

My leader
Our country is divided
Between the haves and the have-nots

The gap between them is exorbitant
It needs to be airtight
Take your country to its place
Where it used to be an example
You must have what it takes
Please take my words

Mr. President
Never give too many promises
Sometimes, they're hard to fulfill
Never say many words
They are easy to forget
Learn from the past
Especially on the issue of promises
Do what you think is right
Then let the citizens decide

Madam President
You're vied to rule a wrecked country
Yes, the country in shambles
Where corruption is in the upsurge
Everybody feels its ripples
Yet people seem to still have reliance
In their leaders they have faith
Leaders shouldn't let them down

Many countries are crises
Even birds truly know what this is
Crimes are exponentially on the rise
Such can't be what people voted for

Honorable president
Drug trafficking is now alarming
Smuggling so, too, is disturbing
Impunity is endemically damning
We need high standards
To see to it that such evils are uprooted
Never look the apes in the faces
Please make sure everything is deconstructed

I know as you do
This is nothing new to you
Since criminality became means of earning
Our people lost the motivation for work
Since drug trafficking became the means of making a killing
Our youths stopped liking school

Africa's name has always been tarnished
Yes, drug trafficking has tarnished it
Corruption has tainted it
Nepotism so too has
Nihilism as well has
Our name needs a facelift
This is our noble and only priority

Madam President
You need to be fast in your methodology
You need to take a tough stand
I like a silent attitude
A smart lioness catches then roars
Please keep this approach as you guide the mass

Mr. President
Remember the story of Mr. Clean
Yes, I am talking of Mr. Clean
When he came to power he's really clean
Wait, there's still more about Mr. Clean
When he left he's no longer clean
He was as tainted as a glutton

A true leader must be spotless
He or she makes sure to exit office sparkling
A true leader maintains political asepsis
It is the only thing that always is promising

My leader,
I don't want this to happen to you
Yes, a void what happened to Mr. Clean
Again, it is upon you
You know everything
You saw everything
A fool is the one bitten twice in the same hole
A true leader is always smart and humble
He or she must triumph
However, everybody must be reminded

It is easy to become a letdown
God forbid this should not happen
Again, when it does happen
The letdown receives blames
Those that surround him or her
Some will rock the boat
Then, they will abandon him or her

A visionary leader must know too very well
Presidency is a sacred call
The office must be kept above all
Making sure no ill deals
This way one leaves the legacy that's shiny

Keep friends and relatives out of your office
State business is yours
Theirs is waiting like any citizens
Leaders are but temporal denizens
In the office of the citizens
Never allow them to dog your legacy
Those abusing the high office
Most of them leave worrying about their future

Mr. President
I know you; as well, you know my friend
There is life after presidency
Serving with excellence
Does give the person assurance
Yes, it offers real assurance in the future

Those who have been in public service for long
Must not be accused of doing anything wrong
True leaders maintain a shiny record
This way their countries sail through
However one must notice
There are many temptations in the high office
Some will like on it to capitalise
They'll want to quickly make a killing
Sans knowing
They make their future messy

One must have heart and reliance
To keep integrity high as usual
The foundation that one lays
Helps even those who'll take over thereafter

Seeing you in such a high office
Many will like to befriend you
My friend, mind you
They do not want you
They want to trade you
Once you are in the hot soup
They will want you to escape
They will abandon you
It will sadden you
Being left at the hour of need

Mr. President
Some'll approach you through your wife
No doubt; your wife will surely become a toff
Everybody will like to attract her attention
All in all, in the end, they'll leave you a ruin
Say no to such politics of technical know-who
You will end up looking up gung-ho

You know how the first NGOs become a fashion
In Africa nowadays this is a fashion
Never allow this under your administration
Those who allowed this paid dearly
Shiny legacy is more important than such dupery

Your wife is a consort
They may call her first lady
She needs to tame her heart
They'll come with a lot of dupery
If she buys in such a flattery
Believe ye me you are done
Never allow anyone
They all aimed at using her and your office

I guess you adore those with integrity
Their spouses didn't have any NGO
Please remind your wife more and more
She must fear having an NGO
Let her tame her ego
Let her do it this from the time go
For, once the time in office lapses
It leaves one in a no-go
His legacy is more than an NGO

If you want to know what I mean
Compare those who had NGOs
Those who refrained are dearer
Those who succumb now feel bitter
Yes, NGOs serve myopic needs

For myopic ones it is a fact
Such NGOs are important
For money they'll print
The coins they will mint
Again, they forget that
As the office they vacate
They'll still need respect

They need security based on accountability
But no based on favourability

The NGO tempts one's ego
This is why I hate the 1st NGO
It is not necessarily that one must have an NGO
The NGOs are bongo-bongo

The citizenry hates the first NGOs
Since their inception
The citizenry has never favoured them
They look at them
Like conduits to exploit them

A true leader is a hard worker *per se*
He or she needs to inculcate this in others
Yes, one's proves to be a good administrator
One needs to be a facilitator
All those under one's watch
This they must highlight
One must never badge to fire
Those that do evil things
They better go haywire
Than a leader to end up in a quagmire

Look at most of African founders
They doubtlessly did big things
It isn't easy to list down their undertakings
All know what they did to deserve approbations
Everybody can do the same things
Step in their shoes and follow their directions
Due to what has been happening

Africa needs leaders with determination
Leaders who can return such wonderful times
We need to go back to times
When people didn't worship material things

Africa had the giants
Julius Nyerere of Tanzania
Kenneth Kaunda of Zambia
Let us honour Patrice Lumumba
And Kwame Nkrumah
Such were the giants
That walked the earth

Remember Nelson Mandela?
What of Dawda Jawara?
Do you remember Sir Seretse Khama?
What of Sir Abubakar Balewa?
Such are our the beacons for Africa
We must honour their legacy

Founders' legacies are a lesson
You can go into it and learn
Yes, their legacies are classic
Their acts are truly epic
True leaders must go there and get a lesson

Those founders were selfless
Everybody knows this
They sent all of us to the class
They wanted to have educated masses
We need to emulate their legacies
This way, we can pull Africa out of miseries

Many were good administrators
So, too, they were honest
Such heroes can act as mentors
Importantly, nobody should be a dictator
Again, it is better to be called a dictator
When you sting on those who don't achieve
So, whoever that goes back to their archives
I'm sure, one'll get some nuggets

Madam President
Take the country back to that era
The era of self-reliance
Though we're living in a changed era
There are still things with relevance
There is plethora
That we can take from that golden era

Africa needs a saviour
Africa needs someone to reclaim its honour
Anybody stands a chance of being that saviour
Africa needs a consoler
The one that brings it together
It has suffered from dividers
Again, all depends on that individual
If one wants to leave a shining legacy
Must take this challenge seriously

Africa has for long been on an autopilot
It deserves now to have a hard-working pilot
A real leader is that pilot
Who can steer our aircraft

Must go sit in the seat however it is hot
One must give it a shot
I'm sure one will perform better

Africa is at the crossroad
It is no longer respected
Graft has stolen its good name
One must reclaim this name
One must restore its fame
Africa needs to be back in the good eyes of the world
Yes, if we decide
We can clean our tarnished forename

Honourable president
You need to take a firm stand
Our country needs that surely
Crimes should be punted practically
Apply the same zeal you apply on critics
We see them ending behind bars

A leader is like a new pearl for the people
They pin their hopes on him or her
If one takes this to a very high level
One can prove to be noble and believable
One must show that he or she's reliable
One must live up to his or her potentials

Good leader,
Admit when you make mistakes
Yes, we all make mistakes
Even when your advisors differ with you
Please understand that you are a human being

That's capable of making mistakes

All that people need is hope
Yes, they're looking for hope
Truly, leadership is about hope
Yes, it is the business of hope
In you people have hope
So, please don't let them down

You promised not to let citizens down
Please don't let them down I say
This is the only surest way
Through which you can meet their expectations
People have more, and of course, high expectations
This must feature high on your agendas

People want to see food in the stalls
They all need food on the tables
Yes, they want to see their kids going to school
People want jobs to make their lives worthwhile
With sane and sound leadership these goals are achievable
So, make the country habitable as you lead by example

I know the hardship of the job of leading
Yet, whoever seeks it does so willingly
Leadership is dead demanding and challenging
The economy is currently tanking
The national debt is hopelessly swelling
I can hear people loudly lamenting
Yet again, I may urge comfortably
One must restore people's hopes
People need the leader of confidence

They abhor a hopeless one

Truly presidency is not a burden
Again, presidency needs no burden
It needs a keen and suitable person
For all have expectations
They expect one to move them from desperation
Yes, a leader is a focal point of the attention
A leader is watched by the whole nation
Again, if one uses his or her noble know-how
Indeed, the future becomes wonderful

One must sincerely and openly declare wealth
Transparency is but leading by example
Nothing should be left underneath
One must be as open and as transparent as possible
All one has underneath should be brought to the fore
Whenever one sets this precedent
By openly declaring one's wealth
All officials will emulate it
Voters will like it
The nation will move forward

Honourable president
Please work hard with dedication as you promised
I still remember your promises when you were firstly
introduced
Keep this at heart as you seek to mend fences
Remember to look back whenever you plan to advance
Looking back is the accelerator and a good reminder

Do you remember what is stipulated in our constitution?

If anything, this is one of the things people want to see in
leadership
The constitution talks about equality
Are we truly equal?
Are the high and the mighty equal with paupers?
So, please rekindle the fire of having the constitution upheld
The constitution of the country must be respected
Let it treat all people including you equally
Nobody should be above the constitution
Everybody must be under it
Yes, the leader must uphold the constitution
You promised to be the servant of the people

Yes, you promised to be people's servant
Don't change and become their master
Make sure you keep the mantra
For, a servant is what the nation wants
If you, indeed, become a servant
Your reign will be glorified
Even after you exit the office
Your name will be precious

Honourable President,
You said you want to be people's servant
Can a people's servant be above the law?
It is only the master that is above the law
So, please put your words into actions
Show us that you're a people's servant

Make corruption your number one nemesis
Again, try to avoid doing some mimesis
Don't say that and do this

You must make an analysis
Of what is in place
So, too, scrutinise what is amiss
By doing this
Surely honourable president
You'll the best president
You will be different from the dogs
The ones that ate us
The ones that vended us

An active leader must not waste time in office
So, too, one must avoid becoming a holidaymaker
Penny-pinching is an inspiring legacy
Becoming a traveller is worse
It destroys public coffers
Africa has many globetrotters
They ruin their countries' coffers
Then, they do not care
Why should they care?
While they have the paupers to pick up the tab

Our house needs to be in order
Yes, this doesn't need a seer
Everything is in disorder
Please put our house in order
Resume the code of conduct
Resume accountability

Put forth your policies
Let the people know your plans
With their support and understanding
They'll be ready to support them

Collectively you will implement everything
Then, the country will move forward

You know your country very well
You've been working for a long time
You, too, know its problems well
They were not created at one time
Take them on without wasting time
The search is about the leader who can see us through

People need a trailblazer
The one who can revive their economy
The one who can put people to work
I don't have this to refuse
That many people are out of work
They need their lives back
By being able to work
It is only through work
A leader must revive the economy

Honourable president
You need to rightly do your homework
To see to it you make people work
We need a working nation
But not a begging nation
We've been a begging nation for long
This should come to an end

We're endowed with immense resources
Make them the capital
Resuscitate dormant factories
Let them work outstandingly

I know you can
Yes, you can
Please don't let us down

You promised to be a go-getter
Yes, this promise is better
Make our lives better
Never allow it to falter
Try to be as much as an achiever
Yes, you can be even a do-gooder
Take this moment
Put it at work
Surely, you'll reap the rewards

A good leader must be good at listening
So, too, he or she must be good at following up
With such engaging style
Africa can gallop
Believe me, nations can triumph
Africa has been walking for long
Now needs to leap not limp

Honourable president,
You know where our money's sinkholes are
Yes, you know even who the culprits are
Take them on without any mercy
Deal with them with all urgency
Put a new way of doing things in place
This way our country will gain prominence

Form a sizeable government
Stop rewarding friends
Stop profligacy
Yes, avoid extravagancy

I've already mentioned graft
Yes, graft destroys the economy
So, too, does bad planning
I must note the habit of stealing
Bring culprits to book without hesitating
Send them a shock and a pain
For others this will be a good lesson

We want to hear them complaining
We would like to see weeping
Make sure that you do something
Yes, something that'll give them a warning
We want to see them going
Yes, for, they should go to the dungeon
As they pay what for what they've done

Take on all sharks
Take on all crooks
Be they government execs
Even if they are people of business
We want to see them packing
We want to see them trembling
As they holler and shriek
This is what we expect
Yes, we need to see you doing that

Drug traffickers are another menace
Please, take no chance on these felons
We want to see you as you pounce
Make their nights sleepless
Show them how things have changed
Make sure all stone are turned
Let everybody declare his or her affluence

Honourable president
There is a group of people I love to hate
These are drug traffickers
They've poisoned our youths
Looking at them you can't believe
Their sacrilege badly numbs the mind
Given that this crime is obvious
It is time for all of us
To stand and say never
Let's say never to this criminality
Everybody say never to this brutality
Let's raise our voices
So that victims can have a voice
You will easily nab drug traffickers

All those who thought are above the law
Must be shown the wrath of the same law
One must govern by law
Just show them the raw law
Make them gnaw
Yes, we want the rule of law
Nobody should be above the law
How can a weak human be above the law?
Being above the law is fraudulent

Yes, the nature of our humanity
Makes us vulnerable
Our lives become pointlessly miserable
You too must be under the law
Follow the constitution from its preamble

We're tired of *holier than thou*
Enough is enough
We must really be hard and tough
This way we'll safely sail through
Nobody should be allowed to bluff
I repeat though
We need to be tough enough

I heard you saying it openly
You said clearly and nicely
I heard you telling everybody
That people should abide by law
Now use the same law
To make sure that everybody abides by it
Those who will break it
Must receive their rewards

Delinquents should never be free
They'd be in the custody
Let them go there and eat free
As they pay for their criminality
Citizens are tired of impunity
Please never allow it to tarnish our image
Doing so is surely but a damage
Yes, the damage you can't assuage

We need a law abiding nation
Yes, a nation based on culpability
The nation full of probity
This must not be in liminality
We need to see it with it limpidity
So, don't allow any plot
When it comes to culpability
Whoever that goes against the statute
He or she must get a deservedly punishment

Citizens are tired of just the same
Criminals are known by names
Some killed innocent persons
Then, they're freed from being blameable
This is completely unfair
Never allow it to happen again
For, it causes despair

Some robbed our coffers
We ended up becoming losers
Many became paupers
Not just because they are lazy
No, it is because
Those in power robbed them

We see them laughing at us
They stashed billions abroad
They robbed us by hoards
They called them trifles
This indeed baffles
Please erase this inconsistency
We now need justice

Yes, we now seek justice
You're the one to do us justice

I know you know thieves' names
You know them by faces
We want to see them barbecued
We want to see them crucified
This will send a strong signal
Yes, all criminals will get the signal

I'd urge you to change the constitution
The president should not be above law
Changing the law balances the equation
That no one'll get a deal that is raw
A person above the law
Is like finger on the trigger
Surely, it'll fire the gun

Absolute power corrupts absolutely
Never accept such absolute power
It corrupts absolutely
One ends up becoming a loser
Especially when one's out of power
One'll see the effects clearly
It'll affect her or him negatively thereafter
Africa has many power monsters
Those who want to rule forever
Yet, they know they will one day die
Why don't they want to face this reality?

Being a human like others
A leader must do like others

Encouraging them to follow orders
One needs to firstly follow the same orders
This is what we call accountability
Yes, it measures one's sincerity
Based on taking responsibility

Making promises offers possibilities
What we need is the applicability
That can be measured based on practicality
For, having possibilities
Without practicability and applicability
Is as good as having no any of it

You said you won't fear anybody
So, too, favour nobody
Yours is to do justice for everybody
I concur with this line of reasoning
We want to see things happening
We want to see justice returning
So, too, we want to see culprits suffering

Our borders are porous
Drugs are just passing
Fake medication are allowed in
Substandard ones are being let in
For the nation this is dangerous
Make sure everything is changing
Charge all corrupt officials
Those who steal our resources

Take over their loots
Go down to the roots

Charge all plotters
Show them that you're serious
This way you'll deliver us

Take on bribe seekers
Yes, take even the givers
They're all precarious
We need to send them the warnings
They'd now realise
Yes, they'd realise
That there's no more business as usual

Africa has many counterfeiters
They forge almost everything
Close all diploma mills
Arrest all of their beneficiaries
We know them by names
Some are even dignitaries

You heard of the ministers
So, too, you heard of MPs
Those who forged their credentials
Others are still government officials
We want to see them hit the road
They must be charged
So that the courts may decide

Many forgers were employed
Others were appointed
Declare their employment null and void
Let them pay for their misdeeds
Education should be respected

It should be earned by merit

We know many PhD holders
Who didn't get them deservedly?
We want them behind bars
Yes, they must get their rewards
Revamp our education system
Let it gain its lost qualities

Ghost workers are another menace
It has become a disease
Criminals are becoming richer and richer
Simply by employing ghost workers
Soon ghost workers will kill Africa
A true leader must save Africa
This is the very disease
Every leader needs to fight tirelessly
Much money is lost hopelessly
People are getting rich illicitly
Why'd they exploit our sweat wantonly?
Don't we have a government?

Ghost workers rob the nation
They send it to liquidation
Start with them earlier on
We want to hear them as they groan
Please save our nation
From this exasperation

You know everything
You know even where and when things went wrong
Your experience is a weapon

Use it to take them head on
Now you've no snag
We want to hear them wailing

A good leader must burn like fire
For, he hires and fires
Your fire should be feared
Let all criminals get burned
They must pay for the crime they committed
To maximum prisons they must be committed
We need our society to be changed
We need to quickly move forward
Everything must depend on merit

How can we move forward with all these vices?
We need the code of ethics to reintroduce
To see to it that everybody lives judiciously
Yes, everybody should reap deservedly

People should pay tax
Tax aversion should be thwarted
For, without paying tax
The economy will end up being stalled
Income tax and other taxes must be paid
We don't need to hear any pretext
Nobody can run a government without tax

Computerise everything
You'll see how it works
Digitalise everything
I assure you; it works
This is how developed nations work

They've never entertained any joke
Let's make our nation work
Let our leader talk and talk
Then, walk the walk

Let's make our workers work
Farmers should farm without worries
Office workers should work
They should do so committedly
Pay them nicely and timely
Then, you'll reap the rewards

Why'd people torture their heads while they can easily make a killing?
Don't we see people in our streets becoming richer without doing any work?
We know their names and streets and all types of criminality they commit
We know them; and they're everywhere in our streets doing it
If one stops this criminality, then the country will go back to work
Take on such criminals by making all systems of government work
If you do so, you surely will see
Every pauper will have a glee
Let us face it and agree
Can people who get rich quickly and illegally really work?
The answer is obvious that such criminals can't work
Why should they work?
While they have illegal means of robbing innocent folks
We see people going to bed paupers and wake up tycoons

What do they do in the middle of the night to become
nabobs?
Aren't they the same robbers who use guns to ruin other
persons?
Though what makes things worse
The police make many arrests
Criminals buy their freedom and go on with their criminality

You know as I know
Some of our police *eat* with criminals
You know as I know
Some big people sponsor criminals
This must be put to an end now

Don't think I'm making this up
If you want to see what I mean
Please just set a trap
This is when you'll learn
How things are but a cropper
You'll catch many in your trap
Yes, you'll catch many
Even those you didn't expect

We annually lose billions of dollars
Yes, swindlers easily and dubiously make billions
They conspires with government officials
They rob us as pleased
Such things need to be thwarted
So as to see our country through

We produce many minerals in tonnes

Again, what do we get in returns?
Go to all areas with resources
Surrounding populations are living in abject poverty
Why'd they live in such indignity?
While their land is full of precious reserves

We've been free for over fifty years
We need to see the rewards
We need to build the infrastructures
So we must build our citizens
We must invest in our people
And our continent will make great strides

Restore justice for all
Restore equality for all
I say above all
Govern fairly
This is what people need above all

I know as you know; there are many scandals
Yes, they involve many government officials
We want to see you take on these jackals
So as to practically deliver justice

Never look at their faces
Look them in eyes
Even if they are your dear friends
They must face the wrath of the law
We're tired of nepotism
We're tired of nihilism
We're tired of vandalism

I'll remind you of these scandals
So that you can take on them
Many cost billions
Yet, it has taken a very a long time
Without being dealt with

Some involve procumbent
We want all those behind it
To get their rewards for it
We still see them in the streets
As they enjoy their loots
Some are still being emulated
As if they retired
Legally, they didn't
You must stop that theft

We see culprits in our streets
They go beating their chests
They are proud of ill-gotten prosperity
Yet, they are still free persons!
They're supposed to be in prisons
Where they'd serve their terms
We want to see them before the court
So that it can decide on their fates

I know there are still many more
Those that have not yet come to the fore
Dig deeper to the core therefore
You'll unearth many more
Deal with them ruthlessly
Deal with them justly
Most of all, deal with them tirelessly

Hit the nail on the head
As you promised
Fear nobody
But don't spare anybody
Whoever that messed
Must be made to appreciate his mess
We're tired of this muddle
So, please get us out of this untidiness

Another thing for the reminder
Please take this seriously
Remember one important thing
I want to admonish you
There is no business in the state house
So, too, there isn't any in the statehouse
So, please don't allow wheel dealers to turn it into a cage
Yes, I mean the cage of thieves and offenders
Fear them like leprosy

The state house is the seat of power
Yes, it is not a house of commerce
So, it should only deal with power
Tycoons should go to the ministry of commerce
The seat of power should always be cleaner
Please avoid business emissaries in the state house

All presidents are the most hunted persons in the world
Many would like to make fortunes by befriending them
Those approaching them are not good
Carefully, watch them
They want to turn the state house into an impetus

By which to bless their hidden schemas

Some are as gluttonous as pigs
The state house must be for saints not hogs
Never let it go to the dogs
Pigs have nothing to do in the state house
Pigs and other animals live in the cages
Only anointed ones should enter the state house
Yes, the state house is the citadel of the people
True, for the *hoi polloi*, the state house is a pinnacle
The seat of power needs to be respected
Yes, with awe it should be treated

I know and you know too
We've seen people coming to you smiling
Mind you
Not everyone who says "Lord, Lord"
Will enter the kingdom of God
Many will feed you with sweet words
Seeing you is all smiles
In the end, they'll like get away with murder
Beware of those coming smiling
Indeed, they're looking for something
They'll be having their deals
That they'd like you to give a hand in fulfilling
I say this again
Fear them like leprosy

Many will befriended you
Some are related to you
Others will befriend your wife too
You need to be watchful and careful

Once they get what they need
They'll abandon you
Especially when your power comes to an end

Remember those we saw in other countries
We saw them being held above
Some bought even their joujoux
Everything was treated like bijoux
In the end, they were all hoaxes

After getting out of power
Everybody's treated you like a duffer
When you remember all those loafers
That used to fill your sofas
As they sought favours
You end up dismayed
Again, you find everything is over
You no longer have power

Many with bad intents will hunt you
Yes, they always want to get you
Once they fool you
As you get into their ploy
Once they're done with you
They'll start avoiding you
Others will hate you
While they benefitted from you

Many pretend they love you
In actuality they hate you
They just want to use you
Yes, they'll brag they respect you

Others pretentiously will revere you
Again, what they want is use you
Once they get you and use you
After they get what they wanted
You'll wonder to note they've vanished

Currently you can't see the mess
How can you while you're still in office?
When time to call it a day comes
You'll vividly remember these words
When the moment of truth arrives
These words will haunt you
Again, you won't have any time
To turn things around
Once you're done you're done
Pride comes before a fall
That is all
We saw many as they fell
Their lives became a hell
Other died in exile
While other ended up in jails

Getting into power is sweet
However, exiting may be bitter
You remember all those fine moments
All ends up being like dreams
You wish they were dreams
Again, they aren't dreams
They're but true realities

Ask those who faced such a conundrum

They were all the time surrounded
Once power change hands
Nobody does the same to them
Old friends abandoned them
Retiring becomes mayhem
Life become a problem

Whoever that ignores this wisdom
He or she will see it vividly
It takes time to accept it
Again, slowly the message hit home
However when this happens
Power is long gone
Power
Power
Never trust power
Never abused power
Never misused power

Power is like a coat on the body
It won't be worn forever
Sometimes, it can be jeopardy
If the bearer is not clever
Power is like a tragicomedy
It amuses and frustrates
All depends on how you use it

Power over others is a ruse
It attracts some abuses
It can result into misuses
You need to take it with great attention
Power is like an illusion

One with it must be cautious
This way one leaves power with decorum

A leader shouldn't be involved in horse trading
Neither should the leader be involved any evil thing
A leader must be honest and holy
Whenever one exercises power
Power is about delivering
Leadership is not about making a killing
Neither is it for relatives to embark on stealing
Once such things happen
A true leader won't abet them
Instead, he or she'll take on them
So as to remain above misgivings

This is why I warned about first lady's NGO
Let me repeat again
Once your wife creates an NGO
Much money she'll gain
Windfalls will be like a bingo
Power becomes a pogo
Once it is gone one becomes a dingo

Your wife will have tons of revellers
They will follow her in all corners
Everybody will pretend to be kind to her
Essentially, nobody is truly kind to her
Instead, they want to use her
Once you're out of control
Her NGO will become defunct
She will receive no gift
Her firm will become bankrupt

Without watching she will go nuts

We saw the first NGOs in many countries
Those who formed them are now sad
When they fell with a thud
Donors abandoned them suddenly
Once power escaped them
They're now but the things of the past
Such NGOs are now but remnants
Though they used to be monumental
Their sweet lives have become gall

This goes, too, to the first kids
Allowing first families to rob paupers
Is but a temporary bliss
Once one is out of the office
His or her kids, too, lose their faces
They entered in power like doves
They exit like cougars
To be hated like jackals
They will be called jackasses

They robbed many countries inch by inch
They're merciless and selfish
They're totally dragonish
They munched everything
They have tarnished everything
They blessed lawbreaking
In which victims eat each other like fish
They see themselves as they perish
This is nothing to cherish
We need to clean the rubbish

Pish! Everything is now gibberish
Eish! No way can we make do with such a mess
Whereby everything is cartoonish

After having new kids on the block
The old kids hit the rock bottom
All of the sudden
They lose all the fame
That used to go with their parent's name
Even the people who used to flock their home
They realise while all has been long gone

Many'll come to you seeking favours
Others will always try to be generous
Tell them the office isn't personally yours
Tell them the office is equally theirs
Everything should follow procedures
For, making favours is but sleaze

Some of those approaching you are genuine
But out of the many that come are like a canine
When the canid schemes to get a chunk of meat
You'll never see the best of it
Wait up until the meat is under its control
It'll only pay you with a yowl
This is the nature of every fool
Fools are humble when in need
Once they get what they wanted
They unleash their folly

The cat, too, is unreliable

Look at it when asking for milk
It becomes very amiable
It will always become humble
Once it has gotten the milk
It pays through scratches!

Humans are more cunning than animals
Of all humans, fear criminals
Whenever they seek what they want
They care less about trust
They can break all rulebooks
Provided they get what they want
They can break all edicts
Provided they grab what they want

How'll you know criminals?
Don't be cheated by their facials
Listen to them keenly
As you deal with them suspiciously
In the end, you'll know their motifs
They always have bad motives
You need to beware of them

Criminals are useless
They pose as squires
Truly, they're but crooks
They've a very high acumen
You need to be judicious
Their words are so saccharine
However, their acts are loathsome
Again, you will realise
Once you are on the cross

Criminals bite like snakes
My friend, make no mistakes
Once their traps nicely get you
They'll end up betraying you
Theirs is to get away with murder
Even if it means for you to suffer

Such creatures are useless
So, too, they are ruthless
They always create a mess
Then, they want others to toss
Knowing they are crucifying you
Again, they don't care about you

Many if not most will come crawling
Others will come beseeching
Such encounters are humbling
You need to take a warning
Most of them are scheming
They're looking for something
Whenever they got what they need
You'll wonder how they vanished!

The presidency is an institution
It needs much caution
It is but a sacred institution
It attracts admiration
Be it fake or genuine
So, too, presidency has many temptations
Whoever presiding over it
Needs to be aware of it

I know you know everything
Again, you're now in the center
Whatever you're overlooking
It can be easily noticed by any dissenter
Media will be watching anything
Out of it to make an agenda
Now it is up to you
To go back to your library
And see how others survived this blitzkrieg

I don't mean that president should shun people
No, that is not my take
Many will come to you
Most of them will be looking for a morsel
You'll receive all types of people
You'll receive a tycoon even a chattel
All are equally your people
Based on my experience
Many state houses in many countries
Thanks to corruption and other vices
They have become a venue for tycoons
When it comes to the chattels
If you are not immoral
Chattels will have a place
The state house will be their office
If you are corrupt
The state house will also become corrupt

The habit of favouring tycoons must end
Voters should be given the first priority
This is a very important point to take

There's no business in the state house
The state house is the house of justice
Where all those robbed should appeal

I particularly make a request
Yes, it is for poor people
Their interests are ignored
They are made even poorer
This needs to be stopped
For, they are citizens like any others
So, they need development just like any others

When it came to my knowledge that paupers are ignored
Beyond comparison I was saddened
Point blank I was told
That lawlessness and corruption are the causes
It took me a very long time to comprehend
How could humans commit such sacrilege?
Where do they get the courage?
To turn their fellows into items
There must be some loopholes
The governments have to take blame
For excluding paupers from the national cake

The media has it all
It is all over the world
Some countries in Africa are implicated
Drug barons are powerful
They are protected by some governments
They have become governments within governments

Another group consists of poachers

They've decimated our elephants
They've felled our rhinos
Many animals are endangered
Those animals need to be protected
Yes, animals have the rights
People must protect their rights

I hear many conferences and campaigns
They're about preserving endangered animals
What of the victims
Aren't they endangered organisms?
Poverty kills many persons
Aren't they dying in silence?
Why then shouldn't we give them voice?

Selfishness is to blame
Ignorance, greed and corruption are to blame
Complicity and laxity by the authorities are to blame
Why humans should exploit others
Why do we protect extinct animals?
Yet, we fail to protect our sisters and brothers
Yes, we're letting down the paupers
We need to give them the voice

I call upon all countries
I call upon all authorities in these countries
They must fulfil their sacred duties
Of which is to preserve human lives
Paupers are humans
Ignoring them is a crime
This is a sin-cum-crime
Paupers are people like others

They deserve all rights just like others
Being born poor is not wickedness
Poverty is not a death sentence
We need to enact tough laws to combat this
To make sure all are treated equally
Yes, they must have their own voices

Paupers deserve to live like any other persons
They're the citizens of their countries like other citizens
So, they'd be treated like any other citizens
Their rights must be protected
Their security must be guaranteed
For, they're humans just like any other persons
They were born with their voices

The numbers of paupers are alarming
We need to do something about it
Empowerment is a crucial thing
To empower such earthlings
Fighting corruption must be an in-thing
For, it encourages greed for wealth
Countries should fight corruption
Let's raise our voices against it

Let's declare poverty an international menace
Let's join hands to curb this violence
We need to stand together with firmness
Let's show our stance against this malevolence
Violence is violence
No way can it secure any tolerance
We need to take on it without any mercy
Yes, let us take on it mercilessly

We need to raise our voices
For, the paupers have long lost their voices
Every country must protect paupers
Yes, provide loans to paupers
Don't borrow their produces
Whoever that's on the helms
Must be evaluated based on how he reduced paupers

Elderly people so, too, are suffering
The media has never stopped reporting
They have been forgotten
This, too, must be stopped
Let us make this our first priority
To enhance prosperity
Respect and promote human rights
All people deserve their human rights

Insecurity in many countries is now rampant
Many innocent people have been killed
Others have been robbed
Africa is full of many victims
Most are the victims of imperialism
Others are the victims of colonialism
I must mention religious radicalism
That has given birth to terrorism
We need to stop all isms
Yes, the ism of doom

Robbery has become another menace
The police force is among victims

This should be put to an end
Everybody deserves and needs peace
Africa needs security

For, without peace and security
There can't be any prosperity
Even normal productivity
Does heavily depend on security
The nation of insecurity
Is but a calamity

Thugs are operating with impunity
Drug traffickers are operating with impunity
They all endanger our security
We now need security
For, it is our right

Mr. President
Overhaul the whole system
This must be done in a timeframe
In which evaluation can be made
A true leader must stand firmly
He or she must state clearly
His or her resolve to stop this criminality
We all need security
Our economies need security
African currencies need security
Most of them are in a free fall
I obviously see no stall
Why it shouldn't perform well
Make security the priority
We must stop listening to any uppity

Make no pretext
We need our currencies to stabilise
We need our economies to stabilise

Remember small-scale business people
They are always in a struggle
Let them be capable
Of doing their business peacefully
Protect them legally
So that they can contribute hugely
To the economies of their nations

Create employment
Public and private
Create a sizeable government
Make it responsible
Make it accountable
This way we'll triumph
Take it from me
We, indeed, will triumph

Let me talk about the code of ethics
Yes, to develop, we need ethics
Avoid lame-duck's politics
Ethics should not be static
Also it should not be mere statistic
On this I am not apologetic
I say pick the stick
And applies laws to all equally
Yes, everybody must work responsibly

Without having the code of ethics

We'll face the same gimmicks
Where criminals and ticks
Come and rob our republics
Many come as investors
They end up becoming freebooters
They conspire with home pilfers
We have a lot of them in the ranks
Fiercely, we must take on this vice
Whereby criminals get their rewards

As a continent we're tired of begging
Why beg while we have everything?
Begging is not a good thing
A beggar is always looked down
Begging destroys reputation
When it comes to a nation
Begging endangers its reputation

A beggar is not a free person
So, too, is the nation
Begging should not be our option
Working harder should be the one
I know we can excel as a nation
We just need sane leadership
I sincerely hate begging
No country on earth should beg
We've all sorts of resources
Why under the Sun should we beg?
For good we need to stop begging
Let's wisely use our resources

Build sound infrastructure

Invest heavily in agriculture
Be it husbandry or horticulture
Inculcate workaholic culture
Yes, we need the culture of working hard
Whatever that is at hand
It should be done without any conjecture
For, work is our future
Based on our hard working

Pay our farmers well
Incentivise them
This will motivate all
They will work hard
We'll all reap the rewards

Begging belittles the beggar
A beggar is a beggar
Whoever that becomes a beggar
Puts his or her people in a danger
A beggar in a suit is a beggar
A beggar in tartars is a beggar
Nobody should love to be a beggar
Ironically, some are proud of begging

Why burn millions going to beg
Spend the same on projects
Start national ventures
Surely, everybody'll see the results
With the population and rivers
Land and nice weather
African has all potentials to prosper

Begging is psychological
It is mythological
We know leaders who ruled without begging
Why'd we live on begging?
When will we start giving?
For, those who are now giving
One day they will stop

We need to build a nation of humans
But not the nation of chickens
No leader should beg for citizens
As if they've no brains
Make them use their hands
Let them use their brains
This coupled with our resources
We've no reasons to beg

Chickens produce what they don't eat
As they eat what they don't produce
For chickens this is the plight
For human this is but a profanity
So, make our people harvest
Let them produce what they eat

Mr. President
Wisely use our academics
Kick them out of politics
We need to use their abilities
To bring development to our countries
Invest in social services
People need good services
Accountably collect taxes

Taxes will fund social services

Invest in the people
Make the economy stable
Create conducive environment
Yes, suitable environment for development
A leader must have some skills in management
To make the country will forge ahead

Fight economic inequality
That is affecting the majority
We don't want to see the minority
Living in a heaven amidst poverty
For, it will create insecurity
We all know it

There are a couple of things you need to do
Make sure we're self-sufficient with food
Invest in production of food
So as the nation to feed
The nation that others fed
Will never be free

Protect our land
From foreign and home land grabbers
Protect our minerals
They're robbed by criminals
We need to see dividends
That'll increase our stipends
As the nation of emeralds
Our people need to see the returns

Madam President
Invest on processing industries
Everything we export
Must have value added
Yes, revamp our slew factories
Revisit all treaties
That saw our nations being robbed
Leave no stone unturned
Make sure all culprits are apprehended
To the prisons they must be delivered
They must all be charged

Show them that things have changed
Tell them the new era is on the stage
Show them you are in charge
Nobody should be spared
Even if with him you're related

Fear nobody
Favour nobody
Victimise nobody
Equally treat everybody
Accountability must be our embodiment

We want to see you talk the talk
Again, please walk the walk
Send people to work
So that they can build their nation
We need a working nation
Not a talking nation
Whatever anybody promises
Must make sure they are delivered

Whatever one devises
Must be logical and practical

Never reward loyalty
Things should go with merit
Never look at party affiliation
Even family connection
Everything must base on meritocracy
We need to avoid mendacity
It ends up begetting calamity
We need a nation of accountability

The era should come to end
When one messes and is moved
To mess somewhere else
All those who mess should be fired
So that others can get a lesson
With ambition and vision
Such things are achievable

I heard some complaining
They said they're sidelined
They claim they were kicked
Out of eating the national cake
They said it in the open
They say; this is greed

My dear president
Avoid firefighter-like decisions
A leader must sit down and think deeply
Before taking any action
So, too, never reach at any decision

When you're in any mood of a hurry
A leader must cultivate the habit of patience
A leader must know the art of patience
Even if he or she is faulted
One should act calmly
He or she should silence people
Democracy is about this
It is about people's voices
People's voices must be heard and respected

Patience is the mother of success
Nobody's ever regretted for his or her forbearance
A sane leader should never take any chance
Give patience a chance
Whenever there are some issues
Issues that ask for patience
Patience should be the sanctuary

We all wish we'd have everything done
Again, it depends on how we want it done
Better having things slowly but surely done
This way, nobody can regret
About being patient
Whatever it is to be done
We must avoid imperativeness

Mr. President
I don't mean you are impatient
I gathered from the audience
It might be wrong or right in essence
Some people can say you're impatient
Others can say you are latent

You better take notice
For, it doesn't cost you anything

Sometimes, truth is bitter
Again, to me truth is better
For, it frees whoever listens
It empowers whoever learns
I am sure leaders need to listen
Surely true leaders must learn

Never force people to regret
One must show what is perfect
Yes, the perfect choice
Give people what they expect
By entrusting one the authority
Then what is left
Is just prove that you've what it takes
Prove that you are worthy
Prove that you've the clout

Honourable president
Whenever people show you any weakness
Please never hate or persecute them
Instead, work on the aired allegations
Never trade accusations
As the means of solving the problems
Just prove they're erroneous
All humans have weaknesses
This is why I say listen to them
This is the end of my political search
We need to expand the search

Search should go on and on
Till we get what we want

Save Mother Earth

It is no longer the issue of speculations
Neither is it the matter of gesticulations
The world is facing a tragedy
Global warming is a surging danger
All human are in jeopardy
Thanks to this tragedy
It begs a strategy
That'll curb global warming

We're facing many dangers
Yet, I see none of our serious labours
Ecological dangers are real and serious
This is what we need to recognise
The problem begs quick answers
Not just answers but true answers

Mother earth is burning
Slowly, we are perishing
She has caught fire
Chances of our demise are higher
The danger is real and huger
Who'll douse this ferocious fire?
It is difficult to stomach and endure
I see nothing but a quagmire
Soon everything will go haywire
We need to save mother earth

We need her more than she needs us
It is therefore upon us
To come up with viable strategies

Instead of offering lip services
We need to save mother earth

Why are we ignoring our own demise?
Are we ready to perish?
Global warning isn't just a glitch
Its dangers are very high

Scientists have warned,
Not everybody is listening
Environmentalists, too, have presaged,
A few pays heed
Indeed, things are worsening
Yet, people are politicking
Leaders of the world I am pleading
Please save mother earth

Stop politicising on such a crucial issue
Stop looking for excuses
Let's face this challenge heroically
Let's do things realistically
Global warming is here to stay
If we keep on intellectual holiday

We need mother earth more than she needs us
However, she's always been kind to us
Is this the way we reciprocate?
Can't we see such a simple fact?
Please leaders of the world
Save mother earth for your own survival

We need to be serious
Intriguing is ruining us
Our lives are now perilous
If we don't take actions
I repeat this again and again
This is but Armageddon
We need to save mother earth

Try to imagine
What will life look like?
When everything is deluged
Aren't oceans now a threat?
Why are we ignoring such a threat?
We've what it takes
We can avert this calamity

Saving the world is our survival
For, this is but an upheaval
We need to act faster and quickly
We need to work ferociously
Failure to take actions
We are but losers

The politics of the world has failed
Soon our fate will be sealed
If we maintain the state of denial
Does this need any miracles?
Can't we see the perils?
Are we such insane?
Let's act a little bit like humans

Rich countries are denying
Poor countries are perishing
Denial has become an in-thing
Please stop pretending
This phenomenon is looming

Polluters say they've no role in this carnage
Sufferers are but cagey
Again, they are incapable
Of doing something
I see no effort the problem to assuage
In the end, everything will be doomed
Nobody will escape floods
Nobody will endure the hazards
That globe warming poses

This is but our collective duty
Let's assume our responsibility
Let's avoid the calamity
Let's save humanity

Our ancestors left a clean world
We inherited a sound world
What are we going to leave behind?
What are we leaving for the coming world?
Aren't we to blame really?
Let's put some vims

Denial is not a solution
We need to find a resolution
Let's get out of our cocoons
Let's shun pretences

Though we're not all equally responsible
We're equally susceptible
We need to be amenable
Why then become such gullible?
While we know we're vulnerable
Let's save mother earth

Saving mother earth is not a choice
Neither is it an aspiration
It is the only left option
Let's make it our obligation
That needs our submission
Major polluters are openly known
Nobody in invisible in this problem
We better all become responsible
Together we can find a lasting solution

Some don't want to take positive and serious actions
They claim their economies will be negatively affected
They are ready to selfishly and arrogantly kill everybody
Such claims are unreasonable and sheer ingenuousness
Are their economies better than the already affected world?
By the way, whose economy is not adversely affected?

Stop talking about your economies
Such talks are but nonsenses
Stop such supremacy
Let's talk about humans
Your economies are yours alone
Mother earth is for every human
What we need is concerted efforts
That will serve and save all humans

Mother earth is like a boat
On which we are travelling
Whoever that digs a hole on this boat
He or she'll never avert the drowning
Whoever thinks is smart
He or she is but self-cheating
Stop foolish and greedy consumerism
Stop blind materialism
Stop wanton nihilism
Above all, stop stupid egotism

The so-called modern science has horribly failed
Why don't we go back to traditional ecological knowledge?
What is called modern seems to be a wee tad fraud
We need to speedily encompass all types of knowledge
To see to it we save our endangered world

However
The world has moved forward scientifically
We are talking of digital revolution
But the same world has digressed ecologically
We are approaching our self-annihilation
Let us use digital revolution
Let it address the looming problem

Modern machines have failed
They're good at emission
All they offer is but pollution
We see plumes and plumes of smokes
Don't forget our dear and mighty vehicles
Remember our elegant planes

In the list include our smart iceboxes
Aren't they agent of doom?
How many use them?
A few of course
Where do we put the mass we are butchering?

Modern plans have failed
They're good at consumerism
Let's go back to the traditional regime
The one that kept our ecology sane
This is the way to go

Global warming is real
We need to take it seriously
We're on fire burning slowly
The writing is on the wall vividly
Yet, some of us are still opposing blindly
Just soon time will accurately tell

We need hyper-speedier encounter
That will counter the hyper-slow posture
We currently are stuck in our tunnel vision
We need to design an emancipatory mission
The problem we're facing needs vision
It doesn't need trial and error and whitewashing
It abhors witch-hunting

We need to be more competent
Our efforts must be benevolent
We need to work together
We must think about the society
This society is the world

Let's save mother earth

We need to stop tree cutting
So, too, fossil fuel burning
Poor countries must be supported
Polluters must be charged
We must stop overconsumption
That is based on selfishness
Nobody will survive
Those thinking will contaminate and survive
Are but self-deceivers
Such understanding is but ignorance

Let's use our technology
By conserving energy
Our efforts should be about ecology
This way, we'll avoid this tragedy

Resources have been overexploited
Some have been abused
The culprits are acknowledged
Over exploitation
Over consumption
Greed and ignorance
Indifference
Arrogance
Who is to blame?
Who will survive?
Political will?
The state of denial!

As a smart monkey puts it
If you see nothing
You say nothing
And you do nothing
Then you're nothing
You will end up crying
Once the danger start biting
The danger is looming
Let us stop time wasting
Let us stop resource wasting
Let us stand together
Let us save mother earth
Let us realise our future

Africa's Lost Hope

When we gained our independence
That ended up in utter dependency
We were promised of democracy
That ended up becoming nothing but useless

After democracy became amiss
Here we are back to the drawing board
Here we are asking for what were are supposed to have
already had
It is nothing but democracy
True democracy
Democracy without bureaucracy
Democracy without any hidden autocracy

We need democracy
But not chaos
We need to change but not chances
Let's use ballots
But not bullets
Our people need development
But not underdevelopment
They need prosperity
But not poverty
What have the messiahs of democracy brought?

Our people fought for freedom
Hoping they could become free
Now, they are living in fiefdom
Freedom is not here
If there is any, it is for thee

Thee who abducted it
If there any, it is for thee
Thee who abuse and misuse it

We fought to get peace
Where is peace
Is peace the chaos I see?
We fought to get justice
But not getting these injustices
Corruption
Repression
We need democracy
True democracy

Song of Africa

This song is for my mother
Yes, my comforter
The one who brought me here
The one who suffered for me
It is specially and exceptionally sung
It is sung for my mother
This is the song for my mother

I call upon you mother
Mother
This is your song
It is the song sang by your son
It is the song of your offspring
Yes, the song
The song of the betrayed
The song of the tormented
Please listen to my weeping voice
I cry for your solace
Listen to my soliloquy

This song is for mother Africa
My mother
Your mother
Our mother
Mother Africa

The song has no harmonica
It has no cymbals
It has no xylophones
It is the song of agony

It is the song of cacophony
Yes, the song of revolution

With guns they have hijacked us
With many lies they have hypnotised us
With politics they have vended us
With aid they have enslaved us
They have duped us
They pretend to be with us
The truth is
They are against us
They say they fight for us
The fact is
They actually fight over us
They fight over our votes
Our consents
They fight over our resources

With our votes they have sold us
They have devoured us
We need your assistance
Please Mother, send them your curse
May they perish?
All those who betrayed us
May they be cursed?
All those who sold us
May they vanish?
All those conspiring against us

They call themselves governments
While they are gangs of delinquents
What types of governments are these?

While they kill innocent people
What type of governments are these
While they rob our decent people
Aren't they the enemies of the very people?

Some have been in power for decades
Without having anything to offer
All they care about is power
Even if it comes by committing murder
Many think of dying in power
If they had power
They would take their power
When they are put in the grave
If they were brave
They would not cling to power
Given that they are power hungry
They rationalise things like animals

For them, everything is about power
They have reached the limit of thinking
They have done nothing
If there is anything they have ever done
It is nothing but killing
Robbing
And corrupting

Some call themselves liberators
While they are but mass murderers
Some are tribal lords
Others are warlords
They are but brigands
Those who hijacked our people

They preach nationalism
Underneath they do tribalism
They preach pacifism
Behind the curtain is violence
When they say peace
They mean peace for them to rule
When they say peace
Peace for them means conspiracy

Mother
They have taken us for a ride
This has been going on
It started a long time ago
We are fed on
They just come and go
We are tired of this felony
Mother,
I cry for you
Africa
I cry for you

You were condemned based on the colour of your people
Evil people heartlessly and dubiously turned you into a
landfill
They turned you into a dump for all sorts of garbage
You have known nothing but carnage after carnage
Your vibrant culture have been hewed pointlessly
Your people were enslaved
Your wealth has always been robbed
Mother, now you are but a pauper
The lives of your people have become but a sinister

Poetry is my weapon

Poetry is my weapon
This is what I want everybody to know
My enemies must know
This is my weapon
It is the weapon of my choice
Yes,
My voice

Poetry is a very strong weapon
Like an atomic or a nuclear bomb
Poetry is always aplomb
For, it deals with minds and hearts
Poetry is for a privileged few amongst
Many who love to hate it

I will use my poetry as my weapon
Till I breathe the last
What a peaceful weapon
That deals with the heart
Poetry is not just art
It is indeed, the weapon
For those who are ready to use it

Poetry is but an institute
Yes, it is an establishment
Poetry is not for everybody
Though it defends everybody
Poetry is an art
That needs commitment
Importantly, I must say

Poetry is an emancipatory weapon
Yes, it is the weapon
That has always been used for centuries
As the voice of the voiceless

Home many *illegals* must die?

I have something for devotion
I have some people to mention
I mean those dying at sea
As they close to go to Europe
This is their commemoration
Especially, for all that perished
Those who are stranded
Those who were deported
Yes, this is their commemoration

How many must die?
I need to know right now
Why should they die?
The world needs to know
How many times should they die?
And why should they die?

Why should innocent people die?
As the world just watches
Why the world is standing aside
How many must die?
For the world to awake and decisively act

I am talking of illegals
Or call them illegal immigrants
This is how they are abusively referred to
This is the language of their tormentors
The language of those who once invaded Africa
They shamelessly call them illegals
This is how they are wrongly referred to

Wherever they go to
Are they really illegals?

Despite offending and robbing Africans for decades
Some Arabs still refer to them as slaves or abid
In the Maghreb they call Africans slaves
Just because they once sold them
Such human traders fail to understand
That we still remember their criminality
Should we call them slave traders?
Aren't they human vendors?
What social cannibals!

Yes, these are criminals
The same criminals that destroyed our civilisation
Yet, they arrogantly pretend and tend to have forgotten
All crimes they committed against Africans
They conspired with Europeans
They turned Africans into objects
That they could buy and sell at the markets
Yet, despite all this criminality,
Today they call themselves our brothers
Whenever they need something from us
They call us their sisters
When they need us
Are they really are our sisters and brothers?
How if they sold our ancestors
They are now abusing their descendants
How can they be true sisters and brothers?
While they always treat them like animals

Is it not ignorance and bad egos?
Treating humans like dogs
Even some dogs are better
Aren't immigrants *bêtes noires*
That everybody likes to avoid
How many must die

Europe is reeling now
History has dealt it a blow
Yet, there is one thing it seems not to know
History is but repeating itself just now
What Europe sowed is sprouting now
What colonisation enacted is figure-hugging now
You reap what you sow
There is a question whose answer we need to know
How many must die?

Once Europe exported its agents
Missionaries who preached insults
Explorers doctored and misrepresented our history
Mercenaries overthrew our regimes
Merchants story our verdures
Colonial officers had us subdued
They killed and tortured
Yet, we did not revenge
How many should die?
While the world stands aside?

Europeans missionaries came to Africa
Arab missionaries came with their dogma
They taught us forgiveness
So as to perpetually exploit us

Where is this forgiveness if our offenders are calling us
illegals?
Was it forgiveness or just a ruse?
They taught forgiveness
Now they are practising vengeance
They condemned and insulted our ways
They termed them a disgrace
They did not forgive them

Europeans asserted that they brought democracy
Democracy with conditions!
What sort of democracy is this?
They exploited our ancestors
They turned them into objects
They installed colonial governments
They blessed their fallacies
Up until now, they still hoodwink us
That they discovered democracy!
Did they discover democracy or thugocracy?

Despite this fallacy
We still uphold their fake democracy
Can't we come to our sense?
And say this is but nonsense.

Europe colonised Africa
Its agents robbed Africa
Even those they left abaft
Have never been referred to as illegals
Doesn't Africa feed their remnants?
Go ask Indians
Go ask Boers

How can one be illegal on earth?
Africans believe in Ubuntu
In which all members of society are lulus
Though colonial monsters found us in our sulus
We still treasure humanity
We were guided by equality
This is a cyclical philosophy
In which everything is connected

Remember European missionaries
Remember the merchants
What of administrators?
They all invaded Africa
They devoured Africa
They defiled Africa
Yet, they were all welcomed
Once they were satisfied
They just left with their loots
Their countries became affluent
While Africa sank in abject poverty
They did not bother
Why should they bother?
Again, how many must die?
For human rights to apply

Despite the miseries they authored
Africans forgave them
They left their remnants behind
Aren't they still comfortably live in Africa to date?
Who is discriminating them?
But the same still discriminate against Africans

They don't allow them in their countries
They don't want them in the same countries
The same countries whose prosperity was stolen from Africa

Colonisers forgot one thing
They left other black colonisers
They too exploit innocent Africans
Generation after another

Now Africa is aware of their heartlessness
Africa is now sending its missionaries
It sends hard workers
They are not colonisers
They are looking for jobs
They are not looking for colonies

Sometimes, I wonder
When I see former illegals expelling others
I heard it in America
They want to seal the borders
They are now erecting walls on borders
Yet, they have forgotten a simple thing
Just the simplest thing

Aren't the wall proponents illegal immigrants to the
Americas?
Didn't they arrive illegally?
They did that violently

They robbed the Inuit
They destroyed their spirit
They called them Indians

Just because of their illiteracy
They called Americas the new world
Is there any new world?
They abused their ethos
They promoted white egos
They decimated their populations
Where are American First Nations?
Where are the bison?
They were all killed
They did along their mammon
Again, how many more must die?
For the world to come to its sense

We need to heal the world
We need to come together
Let us work together
We need to admit our faults
Let's face the past evils
We need to confront our past
We need to be brave and honest
To take on the evils colonialism enacted

It goes without any doubts
The crimes rich countries committed
Are but the means that made them opulent
These are the evils that made Africa unfortunate
This is the language I want to catch
The is the philosophy I want to teach
These are the tools we need on which to latch
As a world of sane beings
We need to ask loudly
How many should die

For the world to comprehend
We need to state boldly and clearly
Why should they die?
How many should die
For Europe to get the lesson
How many should perish
For Europe to uphold human rights
Whose right are these?
If they don't apply to the so-called illegal immigrants
Whose fault is that?
That they are inundating Europe
Didn't Europe inundate Africa?
Didn't Europe rob Africa?
Why is it pretending to forget?
Something it committed just yesterday?
Isn't this hypocrisy
I would boldly say it is
How many should die
For the world to see the light

For the Wife (Girl)

Now I come to personal search
The search for someone
Yes, it is this someone
That perfects me
This is the continuation of my search
This search goes back many years
Yes, it is in my early age
Here comes the legend
I started the search
The search for somebody to live with me

As my search went on
I tried to find someone,
With whom in life to soldier on
This is when my search took a new turn
From seeking who I am
To seeking whom I will live with
That's when I expanded the search
The search for a companion

This is not unique to me
Neither is it to you
The many go through such a time
However not all
Most of us do
Though differently we may do
The concept is still the same
The need is always the same
Expectation, too, maybe the same
What a search!

At about twenty years ago
As I did my business a gogo
It was in Bongo not in Fogo
Neither was it in Manitoba
I'd have had dreaded Manipogo
It was in front of my office agog
That is where I saw a girl
What a girl!
She was such a beautiful girl
Indeed, a well-bred girl
"Guess what," I whispered
I said, "Who is this girl"

Do you think I was the first?
Nay, I wasn't
Neither was I the last
Many have seen that
Yet, many'll see that
This is life
This is the tenet
Yes, it is indeed, life

Those who went through this state
Will surely understand
Those still waiting to face it
One day they'll understand
Nobody is smart before such a state
So, whoever that'll laugh at me
He will be laughing at himself

Through me you can see yourself
And through you I can see myself
All depends on the experience
Is it before or afterward?
Whatever the case
That is the real state of affairs

Jokes aside
My heart experienced a thud
I felt as if it was bursting
I thought my body was freezing
My mind started racing
My body was heavily sweating
For, the girl stole my heart

To be sure and secured
I had to quickly decide
Yes, I had to secure the girl
Who wanted to hear a tale?
The girl has been taken

I quickly followed the girl
I remember the day was showery
I cared less about the volley
Soaked as pullet
As fast as a bullet
There I was
Facing my girl

In the beginning I faced some disinclination
I grappled with this tormenting notion
I wanted to make an introduction

Admittedly, I first feared rejection
Yet, my heart had to prevail
Heroically, I approached the girl
Ebulliently, I gave my speech
Despite this strong spirt
The girl didn't buy it

However, I didn't give up
I was completely geared up
To make sure I leave thumbs up
The mission was not for courting
It was for only preliminary spying
I wanted to know one thing
To know where girl lived

Despite the failure of my first approach
My greeting was accepted
Getting hi was a success
Yes, my spirit flew in the skies
Nothing could surpass the happiness
When I heard the voice of the girl

Time crawled before me
I had to craft a scheme
That would see me through
The situation was tough
The girl didn't let go
Too, I didn't let go

I stood my ground
I sharpen my tongue
I felt no fatigue

Neither did I lose courage
"The war must be won"
I told my heart

Over a year in the fight
There came a reward
The consent was obtained
I could now lay a claim

Traditions were to be observed
So as to follow the procedures
Elders were consulted
In order to secure their approval

Blessings were investable
Why making elders irritable?
The situation was irresistible
I braced myself comfortably
Victory was on the sight

Our parents followed the same formula
This path is cultural
Foods and beer are prepared
Elders are dined and wined
The union of two families is declared
Then, the girl moves to your home

Next was the process
Where two families are gathered
They meet face to face
Some goats are slaughtered
Big meals are saved

Roasted meat and fricassee
The tables they flood
Many stories are narrated
Lost friends are united
Then, the first encounter is finalised

As the process goes on
Two sides get to know each other
If there is one of yours erred
It is the time to be penalised
If there's any irreconcilable matter
Expect the unexpected
The process can be aborted
You end up losing a girl

Since that day I was incensed with the girl
No day would pass without wanting to see the girl
And truly, I made sure I saw the girl
Yes, I saw the girl

Folks it wasn't easy
Perseverance is the science
On my toes on my knees
I had to plead
At last, I was accepted
She became my wife

The vows were next
To make sure she's in the nest
Kindly, time did wait
Soon she was in the nest

The girl became my consort
She saw me through it all
She gave me comfort
To me she is the last
Even if the skies fall
I tell you from my heart
Nobody can replace her

We might not be rich
Yet, we've a strong institution
This institution is our marriage
In which we always seek refuge

Happy marriage is a gift
No doubt about that
Getting it is a feat
Attaining it needs gift
A couple has to be patient
They need to forgive a lot
So, too, they need to learn a lot
Learning about and from each other
Is not even that easier

Sometimes, one may fall
Then, you pick yourselves up and go
Happy life is the labour
Yes, it is the labour of love
True love
Equal love
Reciprocal love
Above all
Belief in love

You'll enjoy love

Years went by awesomely
When we started we're two
As I speak now
The nest is full packed
Here we're today
The nest if occupied
We're no longer only girl and boy
We are now good parents

Don't laugh at me please
Don't ask me please
How can a girl remain girl?
Yes, she's always been a girl
She'll always be a girl

She'll remain a girl
Even if she hits eighty
My girl will remain a girl
Even if she becomes a centenarian
She will still be my girl
Don't ask me why

My grandchildren will call her senior
To me, she'll remain younger
Even with wrinkles on her face
She'll still be a lassie
This is the girl I saw
This is the only girl I know
The only one I have
Above all, the only one I love

This is the girl that saw me
This is the girl everybody has
She will be there always

Go look at your parents
You can see it even on your grandparents
Do you think they're as old as you deem them?
Every day they see their primes
They remember their times
When they were young prettiness
Everybody's girl will always be a girl

As old as you become
As close as you become
You remember all events
By days, month, years even dates
Your marriage becomes stronger
You get closer and closer
Interdependence becomes even stronger
You badly need each other

You remember everything
You remember the day you met
You remember the words you said
You remember the street in which you met
You remember the flower bouquet
That day you got married
You remember even how the urn stood

You remember the dress you wore that day
Yes, such immaculate garbs of the day
Indeed, the day was memorably showy

Yes, you remember your company on that day
I for one, I remember the music we danced
For those who hired music band
I am sure they still remember the jingles

You remember unforgiving expenditure
You remember how you pushed the envelope
Yet, you remember everything with pride
You perfected your lives and moved on

Sweet are still the memories of the steps you took
As you joined friends to dance
You remember even the look
That stood in each other's faces
Those sweet words you uttered
Not to mention the jokes you cracked
Sweet are still are the memories of the cake you cut
I remember even my hair cut
I remember how my girl's plait

Your remember even the convoy
The one that carried you that day
I still remember the amount I'd to pay
To perfect this very memorable day
We still make some commemorations
This day defines our lives

I still remember even the beer I drank
I remember well-wishers' hands we shook
Memorable are those majestic steps we took
To cap it all, we still treasure the cards we received
Above all, we still thank God

For all that ever since happened

I remember everything bit by bit
Simply because we treasured it
Essentially, it is about being
This is the nature of every human being

Why do I do all this?
When I remember those who were suffering
I thank God and for such a gift
Why shouldn't I treat this as a gift?
While some people were suffering
On the material day I enjoyed the bliss

You remember those humble hard beginnings
When you quarreled with landlords and landladies
You remember their demands and insults
Now you are in your own house

Marriage is like a library
You build on it everyday
You remember the joy
That day you got the first baby
You vividly see the first day
When your first child went to school
It is as if it was yesterday

Remember the first day your baby started smiling
What about when the baby started babbling
Go forth and remember how you felt
When your baby started stumbling
Remember how you oft-jumped

To avoid the baby falling

How did you feel when you see your first grey hair?
Were you amused or shocked
Some thanked God
Others were worried
Their lives were close to an end

Sometimes, I hate birthdays
Again, when I remember the days
That I have lived
I truly thank God

When you feel you are close to death
You may complain and wish you were younger
Do you remember those who died early?
Remember
Young ones aren't sure of reaching your age
What do you have to live such longer?

Some of us need to see their grandchildren
Others want to see greatgrandchildren
We wish they come and make us complain
However, we need their company
Life is but a very wishing scene
We wish we'd live forever
Yet, we complain about life!

Do you wish to live forever?
Go ask suffering elderly
Old age is not that funny
There are many encumbrances

The search goes on
Everybody can still join
Let's search for a treasure trove
It goes on even one is in the grave
Some religions tell us of the afterlife
The search will never stop
It will always go on
What is there that's waiting for us
Who knows?

Some believe in God
Some don't believe in God
Yet, we all want to do well
Here and hereafter if you will
Nobody wants to go to hell
However, it looks like a Fairy tale

Let me stop my search here
It is not the end however
Everybody will take his or her share
The search goes on up to when you stop breathing
Yet, more remains there waiting and hoping
Who knows what's coming
We better keep on the search
For, it has a lot to teach
Yes, we have a lot to learn.

When it comes to the mysteries of life
We are all facing a gape
We know how, when and where it started
Sadly though, we don't know how it'll end

This is worrying and sad part of it
The many don't like to think about
However, it is always there
Whether we like it or not
It will always be there

Whatever we get hands on
Whoever we feel were are
Everything will come to a conclusion
It is indeed bizarre
When we think of the end
The end without end
The end of end
Our lives are unknown
The mystery goes on

Kings and subjects will die
Presidents and voters will die
Tycoons and paupers will croak it
Animals do die
Insects, too, die
We'll all croak it
Regardless of who think we are
Regardless of what we have
The end is the grave
Yet, the search may go on

The Sun will rise and fall
The Moon will shine and fall
Our end is not the end of all
Yes, our lives didn't mean the beginning of all
From grace many will fall

Others' pride will swell
Yet, we all concur
Nothing is forever

Who knows?
The Sun will come to an end
Will it fail or fall?
Where will the stars go?
Will they fall?
Will they vanish in the black hole?
Who knows?
The good news is
The world will come to an end
Nobody will be spared
All will suffer the same fate
This is what the search is all about
Will we solve the mystery?

Where will the world go?
Religions do not tell
Yet, some know
It will go where it started
Where did it start?
Isn't it from the confusion?
Who can tell with certainty?
Will it be possible in this world?
What of the coming world
Is it really there?
Where?
Is it above us?
Can it be underneath us?
Who knows?

The search will always go on
Let's soldier on

END